Presents

Learn GUITAR 2

Written & Method By:
John McCarthy

Adapted By: Jimmy Rutkowski
Supervising Editor: John McCarthy
Music Transcribing & Engraving: Jimmy Rutkowski
Production Manager: John McCarthy
Layout, Graphics & Design: Jimmy Rutkowski
Photography: Rodney Dabney
Copy Editors:
Cathy McCarthy & John McCarthy

Cover Art Direction & Design:
Jimmy Rutkowski

HL14041755
Produced by McCarthy Publishing®

Table of Contents

Words from the Author

To learn a new language you take small steps, progressively increasing your knowledge until you can speak that language fluidly. Music is the language you are learning and with consistent practice this book will guide you to the next level. In Book 1 you learned many of the important basics to build a solid foundation of music. Now it's time to expand upon that, learning new techniques, concepts and how to apply them. At this level you need to learn the "Art of Listening." It's as important to listen as it is to play. Take the time to listen to yourself as well as other musicians. When your ears hear and understand music, your fingers will respond and play.

Grab your guitar, open your ears and mind and let's play music!

John McCarthy

Icon Key

These tell you there is additional information and learning utilities available at RockHouseSchool.com to support that lesson. Register using the member number that is printed **on the accompanying CD** inside the back cover of this book.

Backing Track

CD Track Many of the exercises in this book are intended to be played along with bass and drum rhythm tracks. This icon indicates that there is a backing track available for download on the *Lesson Support* site.

Metronome

Metronome icons are placed next to the examples that we recommend you practice using a metronome. You can download a free, adjustable metronome on the *Lesson Support* site.

Tuner

You can download the free online tuner on the *Lesson Support* site to help tune your instrument.

Additional Information

The question mark icon indicates there is more information for that section available on the *Lesson Support* site. It can be theory, more playing examples or tips.

Digital eBook

When you register this product at the Lesson Support site RockHouseSchool.com, you will receive a digital version of this book. This interactive e-Book can be used on all devices that support Adobe PDF. This will allow you to access your book using the latest portable technology any time you want.

My Mojo is Back
Shuffle Blues 1 - 4 - 5

Here is a blues shuffle rhythm in the key of "A." This rhythm is a common 1 – 4 – 5 progression. I've included the chord change on top of the staff so you can see the progression clearly. Make sure to use the backing track to create a full band sensation.

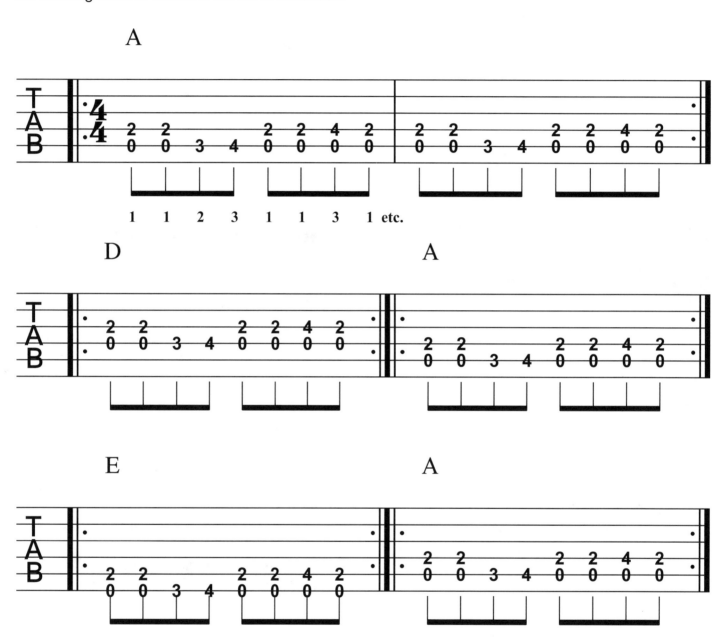

![Music Assignment guitarist silhouette]

MUSIC ASSIGNMENT

Play the minor pentatonic scales on the key of "A" over this rhythm. Start to improvise by creating your own riffs from the pentatonic scales. Play over the backing track combining the lead techniques, riffs and lead patterns you've learned so far to form your own leads. Creative practice will help you develop your own signature lead style.

Bending

In this lesson you'll learn double pump and half step bend techniques that will prepare you to play some great leads. I've outlined a few examples using the A minor pentatonic scales. Example 1 demonstrates the double pump bend. To execute this bend pick the note and bend in an up – down – up motion all with only one pick. Example 2 includes two half step bends, the first with your 3rd finger and the second is a 1st finger bend and release. Bending is challenging and can be painful to your finger tips, so, be patient.

Example 1

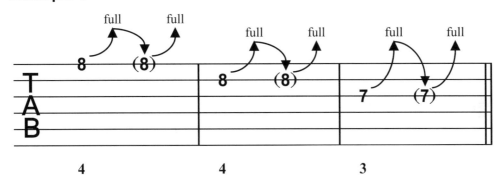

Example 2

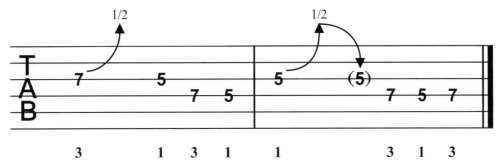

Example 3

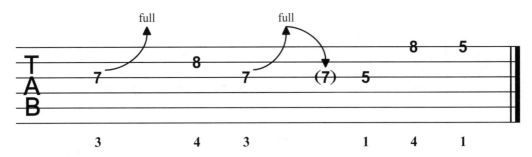

MUSIC ASSIGNMENT

Since bending is a difficult technique, I have designed an exercise that will help you master this technique easier. Choose any note on your guitar as a note that you wish to bend. Play the note two frets higher then that note. This is the pitch you need to achieve to bend a whole step. Bend notes using this exercise across the neck. Although you can bend a note on any string, I recommend that you start with notes on the first three strings, they are used most and are easiest to bend.

Lead Riffs with Bending

Now it's time to apply the bending techniques and create lead riffs! A riff is a single note phrase formed within the notes of a scale. The following are a series of riffs created from the A minor pentatonic scales. Get comfortable using bends, they will add character to your playing. Riff #1 incorporates a double stop (striking two notes together with one swing of the pick) and a 4th finger double pump bend.

Riff #1

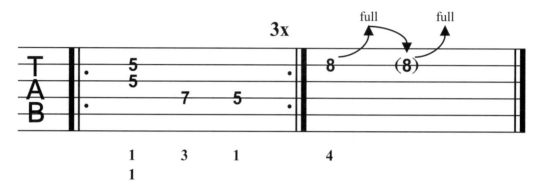

Riff #2

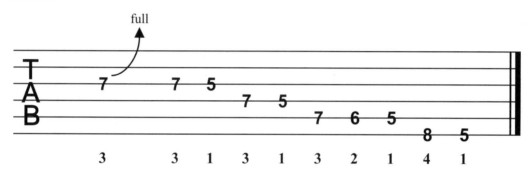

Riff #3

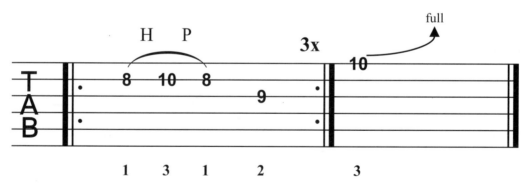

Riff #4

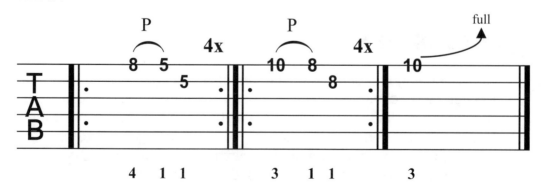

6

Riff #5

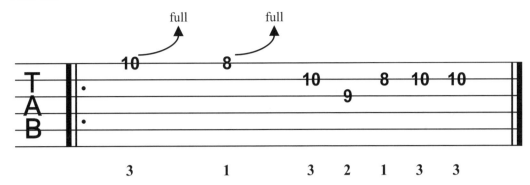

Sixteenth Notes

CD Track
6

A sixteenth note receives ¼ beat of sound. It subdivides one beat into four equal sections. Sixteenth notes are twice as fast as an eighth note. Count out sixteenth notes now as follows:

1 - e - & - a, **2** - e - & - a, **3** - e - & - a, **4** - e - & - a

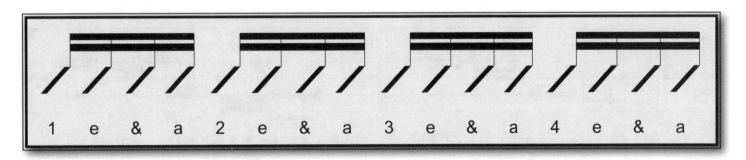

There are four subdivisions for every one beat. Tap your foot down on each beat or number. Now play sixteenth notes with the open low E string using alternate picking. Accent (pick harder) on the down beat to get a true sixteenth note feel.

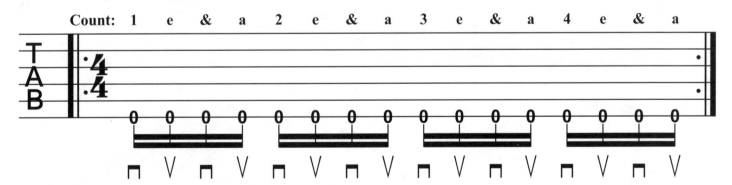

MUSIC ASSIGNMENT

Count sixteenth notes along with your favorite music. As a song is playing, tap your foot and count along using eighth and sixteenth note timing. Get familiar counting these note values because they are very common in every genre of music.

Speed Demon Exercise

Get ready to give your fingers a challenging workout! This exercise is a great one to develop finger coordination to help you play difficult pieces with ease. There are six variations; each variation adds one string to the exercise. Remember to use consistent alternate picking and build speed gradually. Don't hold any fingers down; lift each finger up after you pick it in a piston like manner, one finger is going down while the next is going up. This will develop finger independence.

Play each measure eight times:

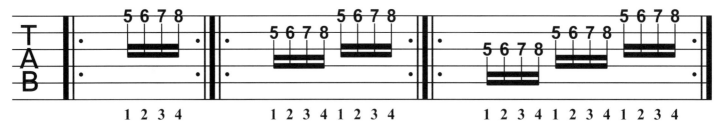

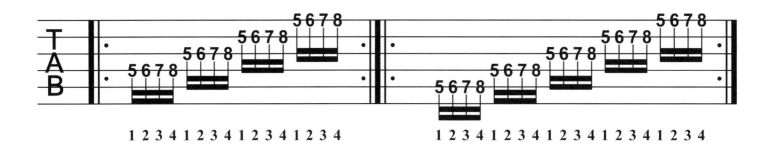

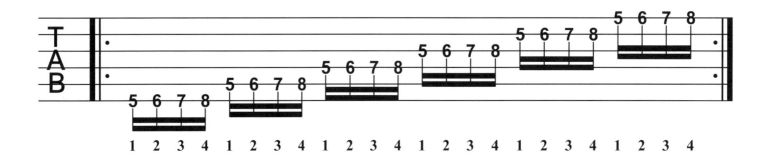

MUSIC ASSIGNMENT

Get comfortable with this exercise and build up speed then try moving it down one fret, starting on the 4th fret 4 – 5 – 6 – 7. The reason to do this is the frets get wider as you move it down and it will be a bit more challenging. Keep moving it down one fret at a time until you get to the 1st fret.

Sixteenth Note Lead Pattern

Now put those sixteenth notes into action with a lead pattern in the key of "A."

1st Position

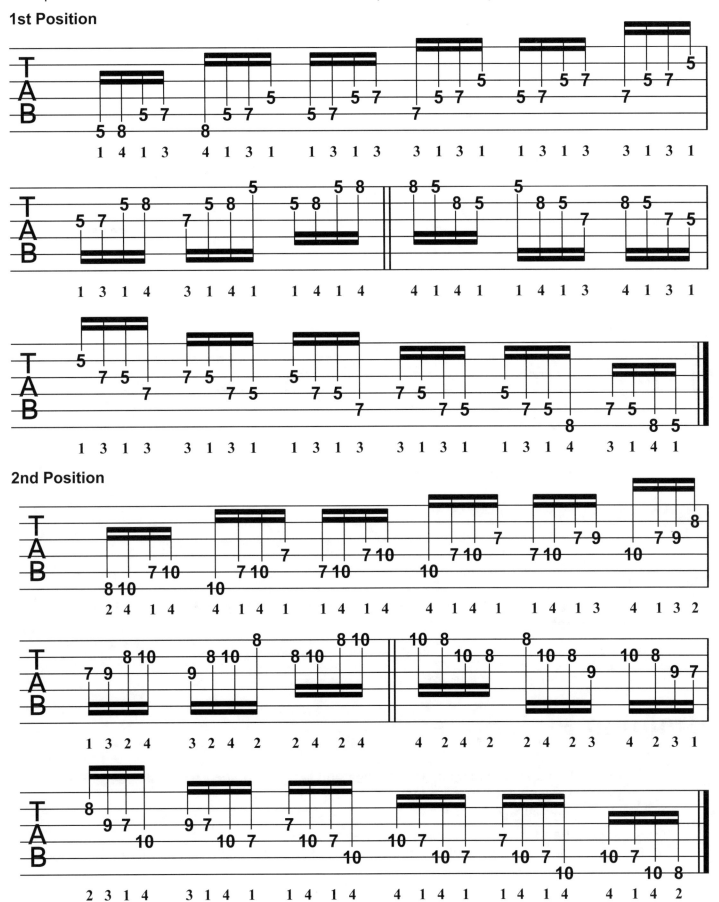

2nd Position

Double Stops

A double stop is a pair of harmonized notes from a scale or chord played simultaneously. This creates a fatter, fuller sound. The following are double stop song rhythms:

Double Stop Blues

CD Track 10-11

The Crew

CD Track 12-13

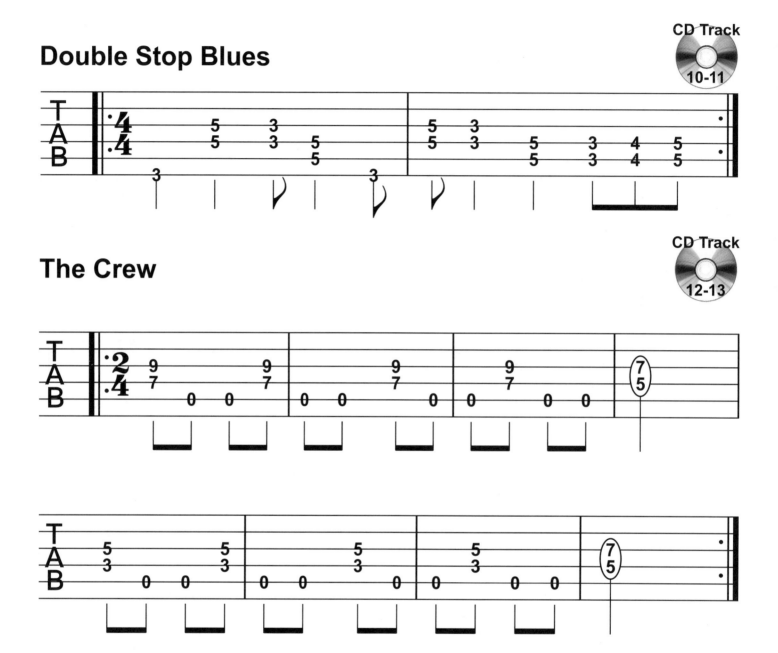

Building Pick Speed

Here are a few tips to help you play difficult melodies and leads with accuracy and speed.
1. Use only the tip of the pick.
2. Use alternate picking.
3. Keep your hand, arm and shoulder loose and relaxed.
4. Breathe, many players hold there breath when playing difficult passages in a song and this makes your body tighten up.

Minor Pentatonic Scales
Key of "E"

SCALE PROFESSOR

The two most popular keys in rock and blues music are A and E. It's easy to change keys with these scales; just move the scale patterns you previously learned to different frets. The 1st scale position always starts on the root note, or the key. In the key of "E" the 1st scale will start with the open 6th string which is an E note. This position can also be played an octave higher at the 12th fret. Play the following five pentatonic scales and pay close attention to where all the E notes (root notes) fall within each position. The five notes that make up the E minor pentatonic scale are E – G – A – B – D.

1st Position (Open)

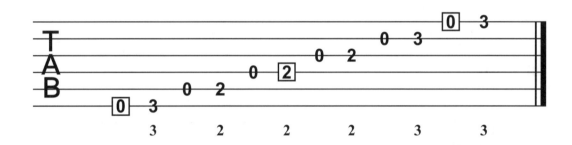

2nd Position

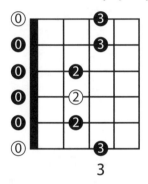

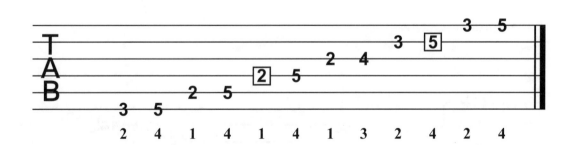

3rd Position

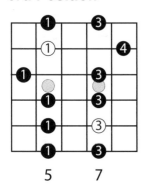

5   7

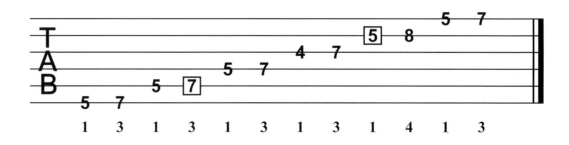

1 3 1 3 1 3 1 3 1 4 1 3

4th Position

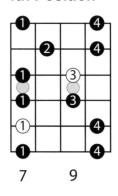

7   9

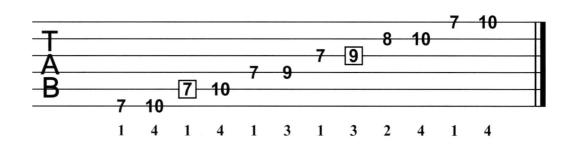

1 4 1 4 1 3 1 3 2 4 1 4

5th Position

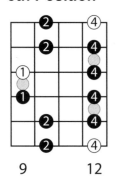

9   12

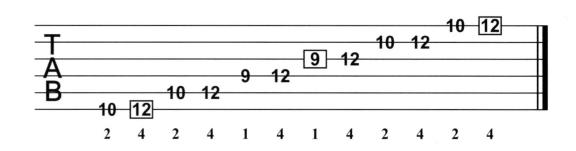

2 4 2 4 1 4 1 4 2 4 2 4

1st Position (Octave)

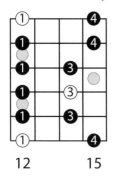

12   15

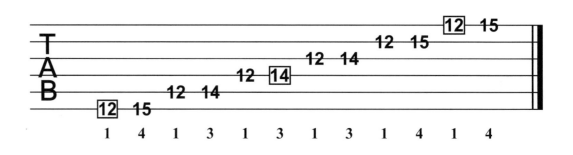

1 4 1 3 1 3 1 3 1 4 1 4

12

MUSIC ASSIGNMENT

It is important to play scales in a creative manner. Below is a basic E minor chord progression. As you are learning the scales in the key of E play them over this chord progression. I have included this progression on the accompanying CD at the end of the 1st Position Octave track.

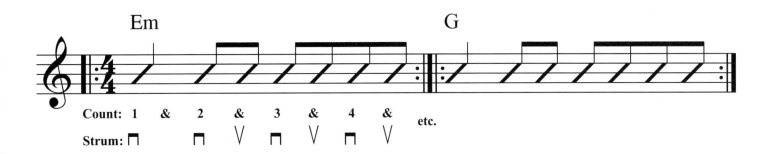

Connecting the Scale Patterns

If you look closer, the five minor pentatonic scale patterns connect like a puzzle. These five scale positions fit together perfectly like legos. The second half of the 1st position is the first half of the 2nd position; and so on, through all five scales.

Look below to see how this works with the scales in the key of "E." I've used a full neck diagram so you can see all the scales across the neck and how they connect.

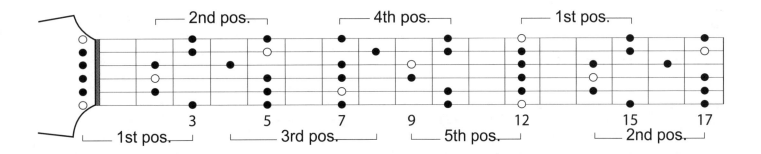

There is a commonality; the fret distance between each position is always the same. For example, in any key the 2nd position scale will always start 3 frets higher than the 1st position, the 3rd position will always be 2 frets higher than the 2nd position and the 4th position will always be 2 frets higher than the 3rd position. Study the full next diagram above and visualize all the scales in this key across the neck and how they connect from one scale to the next.

Lead Patterns in the Key of "E"

CD Track
20-22

Let's play lead patterns with the minor pentatonic scales in the key of "E." Follow the tablature below to play the lead patterns with the 1st and 2nd scale positions. The follow lead pattern is written in eighth notes but you can also play this as sixteenth notes to make it more challenging. Remember to use alternate picking and build up your speed gradually. Make sure every note is played clearly before increasing your speed. I recommend that you use a metronome to gauge your progress.

1st Position Follow Pattern

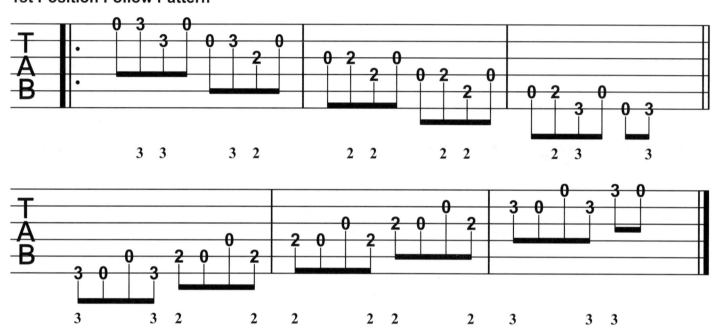

2nd Position Follow Pattern

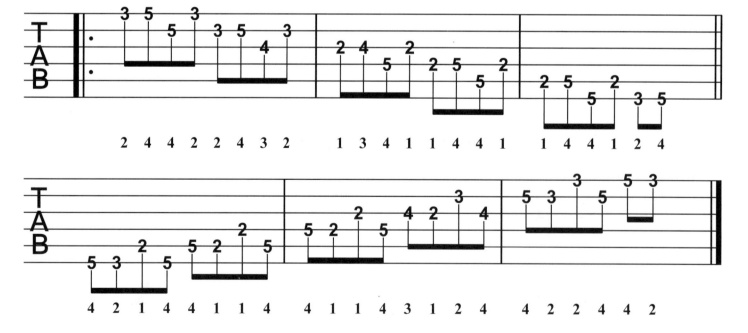

14

This lead pattern uses a triplet pattern. We first learned triplets in Book 1. We will get deeper into the triplet timing later in this program.

1st Position Triplet Pattern

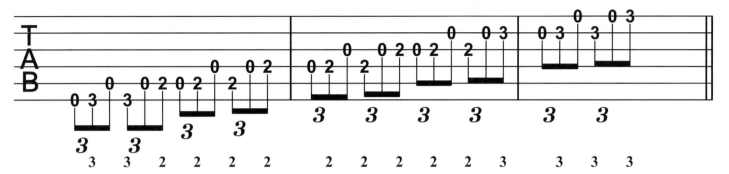

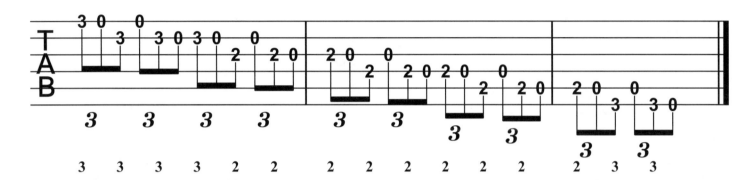

Remember the Day
E Minor 6 - 1 - 4 - 5 Progression

CD Track
23-24

Fret the chord named above the staff and pick the notes separately using the picking pattern in the tablature below. Picking patterns are used in many songs and create a dynamic sound. Once you can smoothly change from chord to chord play this progression over the backing track.

Em - 6   G - 1

C(add9) - 4   D - 5

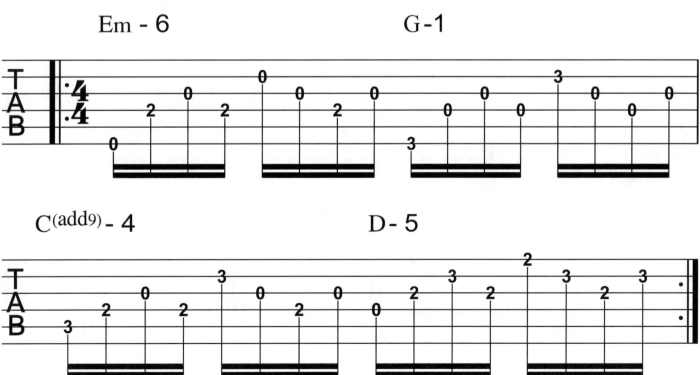

Riff Challenge

Below you'll find lead riffs in the key of "E" that will challenge your fingers. These riffs contain hammer ons, pull offs, double stops and bending techniques. Listen to the audio that corresponds with these riffs to learn the timing and get the feel.

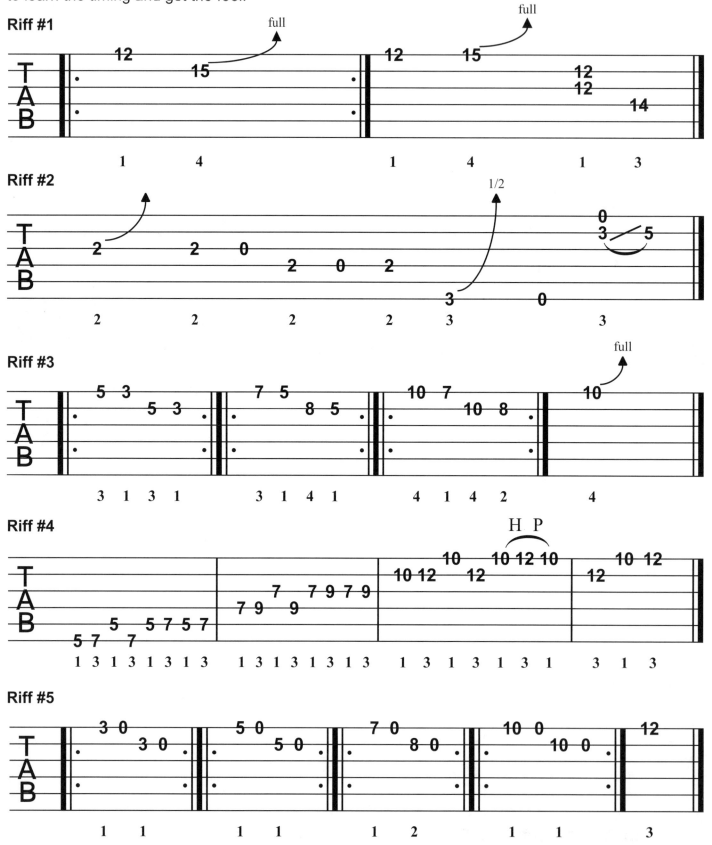

16

Minor Pentatonic Scale Key Chart

You can transpose the minor pentatonic scales to any key by moving each of the five positions to different frets. This allows you to use these scales to create melodies and leads in any key anywhere on the fret board. For instance, if you were to move all of the A minor pentatonic scale positions two frets (one whole step) higher, you would be playing in B.

The following chart shows the minor pentatonic scales in some popular keys, indicating where each position starts by fret. Choose a key from the left hand column and follow the chart across to see which fret each position starts on. Since an octave is only 12 frets, some positions can be played in two different places on the neck.

Key	1st Position	2nd Position	3rd Position	4th Position	5th Position
"A"	5th & 17th	8th	10th	12th & Open	3rd & 15th
"C"	8th	11th	13th & 1st	3rd & 15th	6th & 18th
"E"	12th & Open	3rd & 15th	5th & 17th	7th	10th
"G"	3rd & 15th	6th & 18th	8th	10th	13th & 1st
"B"	7th & 19th	10th	12th	14th & 2nd	5th & 17th
"D"	10th	13th & 1st	3rd & 15th	5th & 17th	8th
"F"	1st & 13th	4th & 16th	6th & 18th	8th	11th

MUSIC ASSIGNMENT

Work on memorizing the different keys and where they are located on the neck. Drill yourself, say you want to play B minor, guess where it is located then check the chart to see if you are correct on location. Do this type of "self quizzing" for all five positions of the pentatonic scales for all of the seven keys given in the chart. Also have a friend or family member quiz you in the same manner.

Bar Chords

CHORD PROFESSOR

The F and Bb bar chords contain no open strings. This means you could play them on any fret on the neck. They will change names as you move them from fret to fret. After you have all the notes sounded, move them up the neck one fret at a time to the 12th fret. These are very difficult chords to play, so don't get discouraged if you don't get all the notes to sound when you first try them.

Quick Tip: On the Bb chord I touch the tip of my 1st finger on the 6th string to mute it because this note is not in the chord.

Bar chords have been used in countless songs, they are very important chords to know. The chart below will help guide you to memorize the names of each chord as you move them up the neck. The lowest note of each of these chords is the root note, or the name of that chord.

Name -	F	F#	G	G#	A	A#	B	C	C#	D	D#	E
Fret -	1	2	3	4	5	6	7	8	9	10	11	12
Name -	Bb	B	C	C#	D	D#	E	F	F#	G	G#	A

Bar Chord I – IV – V Progression

The three chords in this progression are A, D, and E, which form a I – IV – V progression. The rhythm used is: down – down – down up down up. You can make this progression sound completely different by using an acoustic guitar or playing with a distorted electric guitar.

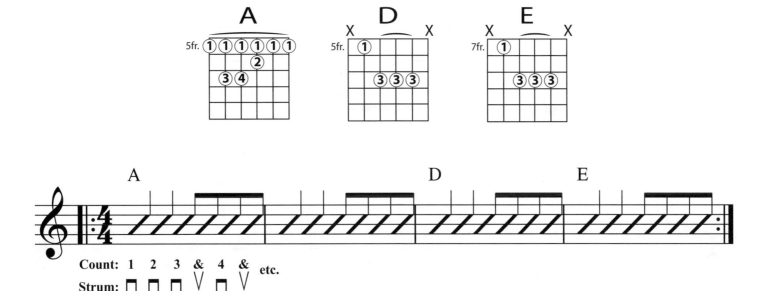

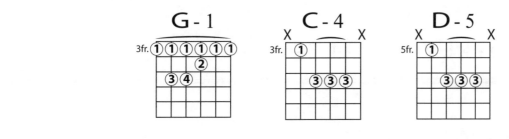

Ramone

Bar Chord Rhythm

The way you strum chords will dramatically change the sound of a song. In this case, the driving downward strums help the song get a heavier rhythm. Make sure to play along with the backing track.

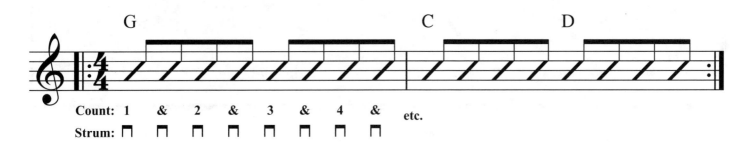

Rev It Up
Syncopated Song Riff

CD Track
34-35

In this song riff play the first note on the up beat or the "&" of one. There is a double stop that incorporates a hammer note, bar your first finger to sound the double stop then while holding that down hammer the second finger. Each measure ends with a quarter and half rest giving the riff a question and answer feel.

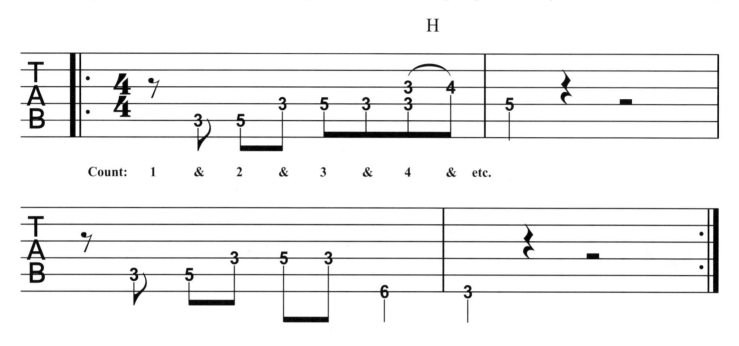

Count: 1 & 2 & 3 & 4 & etc.

Triplet Timing

CD Track
36

Eighth and sixteenth notes subdivide a beat in half and quarters. These are even number breakdowns of 2 and 4. Triplets subdivide a beat into threes. For every one beat, you're going to play three notes. Count triplets like this:

1 - trip - let, **2** - trip - let, **3** - trip - let, **4** - trip - let

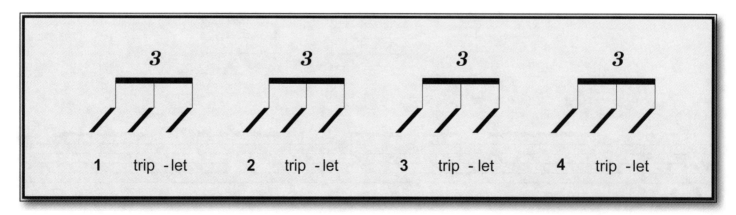

Next play the open 6th string in triplets following the tablature and feel the triplet timing:

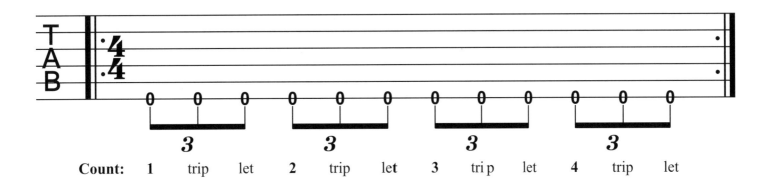

House of the Rising Sun
Complete Progression & Melody

CD Track
37-39

There are a few difficult chord changes in this song, make sure to practice these first to help you play the song in time:

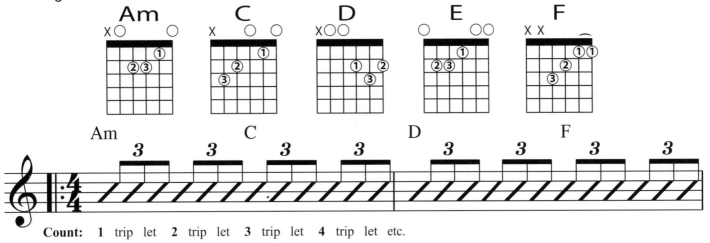

Count: 1 trip let 2 trip let 3 trip let 4 trip let etc.

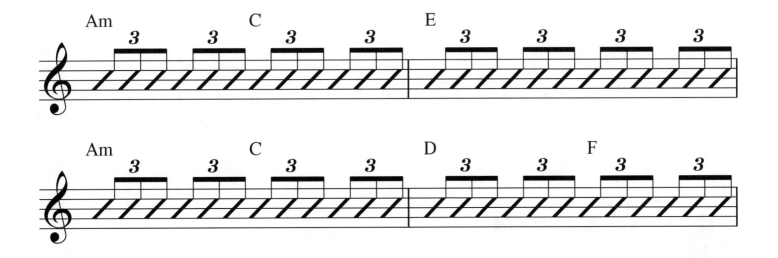

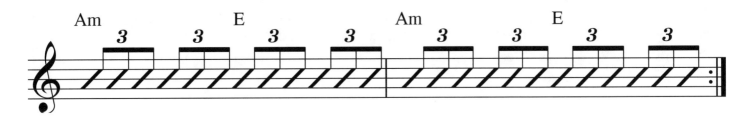

Now play through the melody of the song below. This song is in the key of "A" minor, notice that most of the notes in the melody come directly from the 1st position A minor pentatonic scale. Practice this section by section then put it all together:

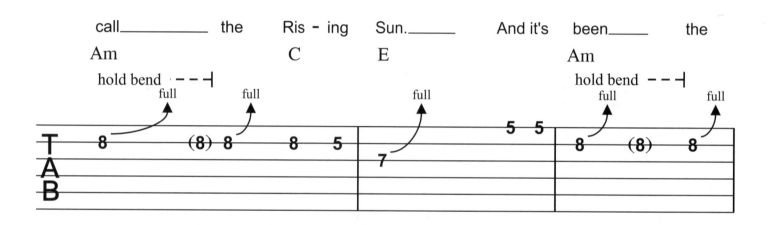

	There	is	a	house	in	New	Or-	Leans	they
	Am			C		D		F	

call_____	the	Ris - ing	Sun.____	And it's	been____	the
Am		C	E		Am	

ruin	of	many-a	poor	boy,	And	Lord	I	know	I'm	one.
C		D		F		Am		E		Am	E

MUSIC ASSIGNMENT

Play this progression and melody over the backing tracks that correspond with this lesson. Once you can play the melody, create your own using the A minor pentatonic scales. There are many easy songs you can now learn at RockHouseSchool.com so be sure to check these out and expand your horizons.

Blues Scales Key of "E"

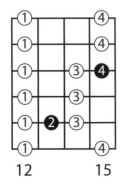

SCALE PROFESSOR

The blues scale is a slight variation of the minor pentatonic scale. It contains one extra note between the 4th and 5th steps of the scale, called a passing tone. This particular passing tone is the flatted 5th of the scale, also known as the blues tri-tone. Using the blues tri-tone adds color and character to solos and riffs. This note is a chromatic passing tone because it passes from the 4th to the 5th steps of the scale in chromatic half steps. Passing tones are used to connect from note to note within a phrase and are generally not held for long durations.

The following five E blues scales are the same as the E minor pentatonic scale with the addition of the blues tri-tone. The black dots in the scale diagrams indicate where the blues tri-tones are played. Practice and memorize the E blues scale positions, we'll be using these scales to play solos in many of the up coming sections.

1st Position

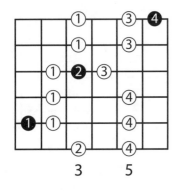

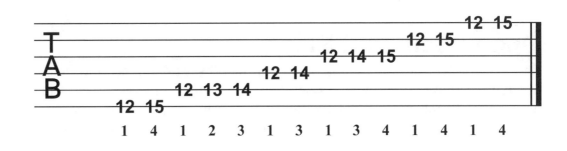

2nd Position

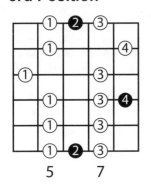

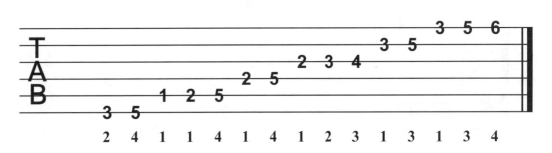

3rd Position

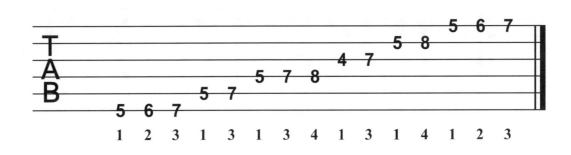

23

4th Position

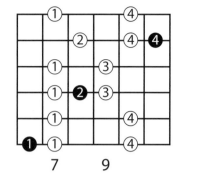

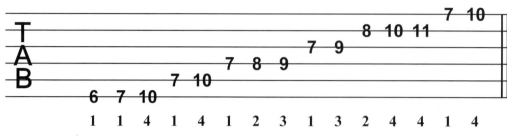

5th Position

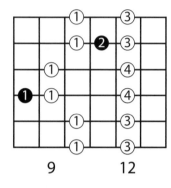

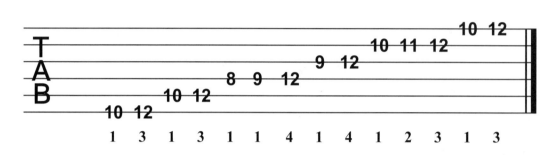

Open Position E Blues

The 1st position of the E blues scale can also be transposed one octave lower and played in open position. This particular scale position is used often in blues music. Playing in open position makes hammer ons, pull offs and trills very easy to perform, making this particular scale a favorite for many guitarists. To play any scale position an octave higher or lower, move the scale pattern 12 frets in the appropriate direction.

1st Position (Open)

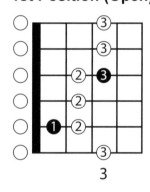

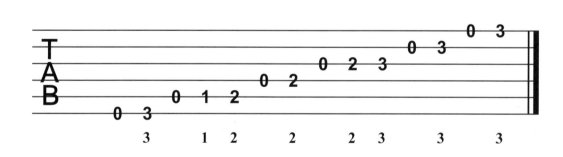

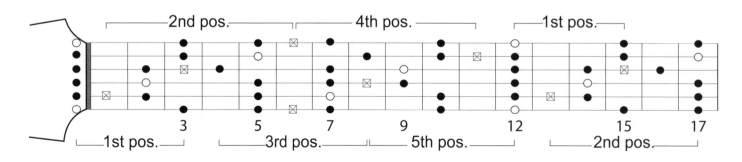

⊠ = Blue Tri-Tone (♭5)

Turn Things Around
Blues in E

The following rhythm is a standard I – IV – V progression in E with a shuffle feel. Play this using alternate picking hitting two strings at the same time with each swing of the pick. The last two measure phrase is a turnaround. This is a riff that smoothly brings you back to the beginning of the progression. This particular turnaround is descending a chromatic riff leading back to the V (5) chord, B. Practice the rhythm along with the backing track, then improvise over it using the E blues scales.

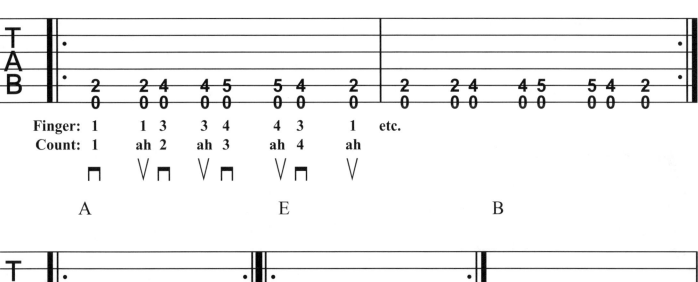

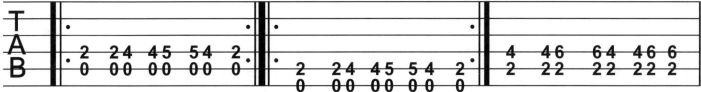

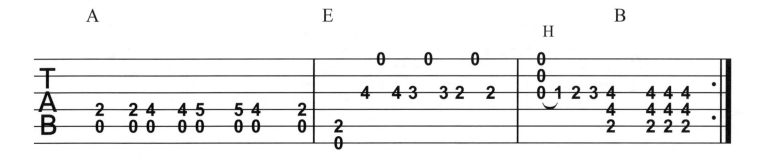

MUSIC ASSIGNMENT

As you learn this rhythm memorize where the chord changes are. Be able to anticipate the upcoming chord change, this helps when you are improvising. A great lead guitarist listens and follows the chord changes and doesn't just play over the rhythm blindly. When you are comfortable playing the rhythm, improvise using each of the five E blues scale patterns over it. Mix up the notes and create leads and melodies.

Slides

In the following example, slide from note to note without lifting your finger off the fret board. The "*sl.*" above the staff indicates a slide and the line between the notes shows the direction of the slide (up or down the neck). You can perform slides using any finger, but you'll probably use first and third finger slides more often. These examples come from the first three E minor pentatonic scales:

MUSIC ASSIGNMENT

Apply the slide technique to your minor pentatonic scales. Within each position slide up and down the notes on each string. Sliding can be a great way to transition from one scale position to the next. The following examples move through several E minor pentatonic scales.

Example 1

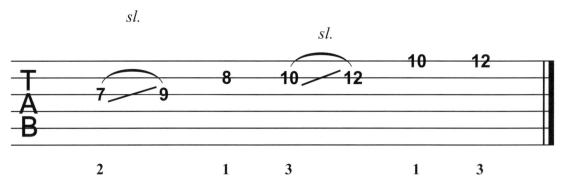

Example 2

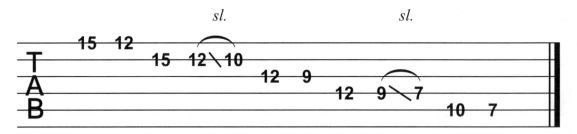

Blues Lead

Here is a complete blues lead that comes from the E blues scales. This lead can be played over the "Turn Things Around" progression. Follow the chord changes above the staffs to help with the rhythm and phrasing. This lead incorporates many different types of bends as well as hammer ons, pull offs, and slides.

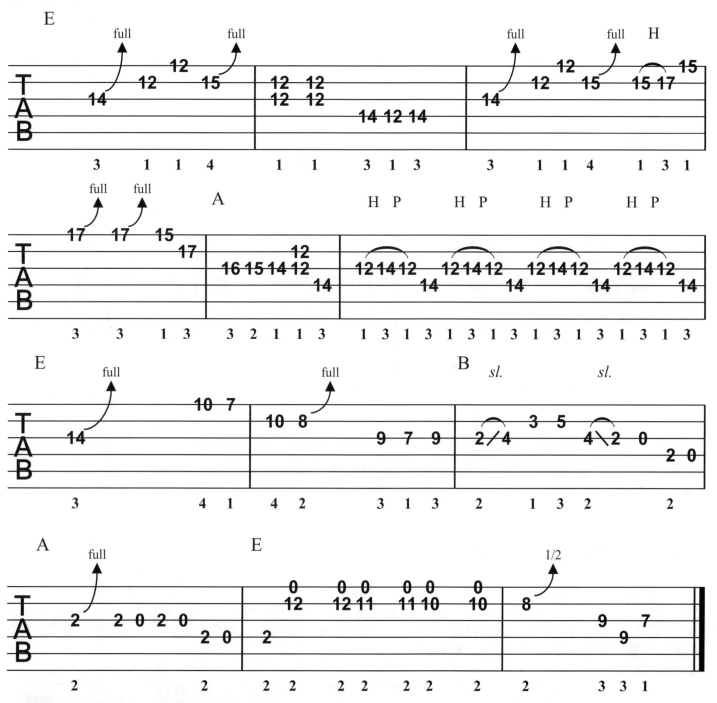

MUSIC ASSIGNMENT

Once you feel comfortable playing this lead, branch out and create your own leads and riffs using the blues scales. Really "feel" the blues emotion when you are improvising. The blues is all about raw emotion.

Notes on the Guitar

Using the chromatic scale and the names of the open strings you can learn the name of any note on the guitar. It's very important to memorize the note names to help as you study how chords and scales are formed.

Below is a complete neck diagram showing the names of every note on the guitar. Start with each string open and move one fret at a time up the neck to the 12th fret. Say the name of each note out loud. Once you have practiced each string several times you are ready to move on to the next part of this lesson, the music assignment.

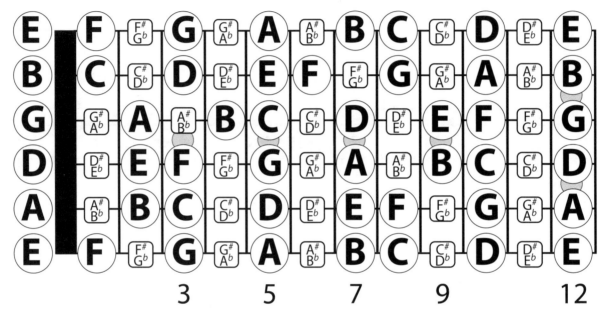

One thing to note, the guitar repeats its notes after the 12th fret. This is why most guitars have two dots at the 12th fret. For example, the open 6th string is an E note when you get up to the 12th fret it is an E note again. The 6th string 1st fret is an F note, 12 frets higher on the 13th fret is another F note.

MUSIC ASSIGNMENT

Below is a series of string and fret numbers. Your assignment is to find the name of each note without using the chart above. You need to be able to find the name of any note just using the open strings and the chromatic scale. I've given you the first answer as an example.

1. 1st string 7th fret – answer B note
2. 4th string 3rd fret –
3. 2nd string 8th fret –
4. 5th string 5th fret –
5. 3rd string 10th fret –
6. 6th string 5th fret –
7. 2nd string 3rd fret –
8. 4th string 9th fret –
9. 3rd string 4th fret –
10. 1st string 3rd fret –

First & Second Endings

Sometimes the composer wants to repeat a section in a song and add a different ending. These are called first and second endings. First and second endings are notated by numbered brackets over each ending. The endings can be any number of measures in length. In the example below each ending is one measure in length. Note the repeat sign between the endings. This means that you play through ending one, go back to the beginning play up to the first ending, skip the first ending and play the second ending. Play through the example below. In the next lesson you will use first and second endings within a song.

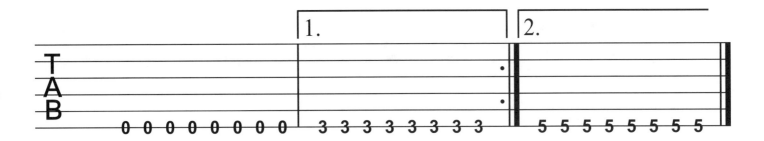

Greensleeves

CD Track

51-52

The melody and rhythm lines are presented in this lesson separately. Play them both with the backing track. The melody is in the key of "A" minor and most of the notes come directly from the first minor pentatonic. The rhythm can be played two different ways: you can use traditional finger picking or a hybrid picking technique. For hybrid picking use your pick and middle finger to pick when two notes are together. Use the pick to hit all the single notes.

Greensleeves Hybrid Picking Rhythm

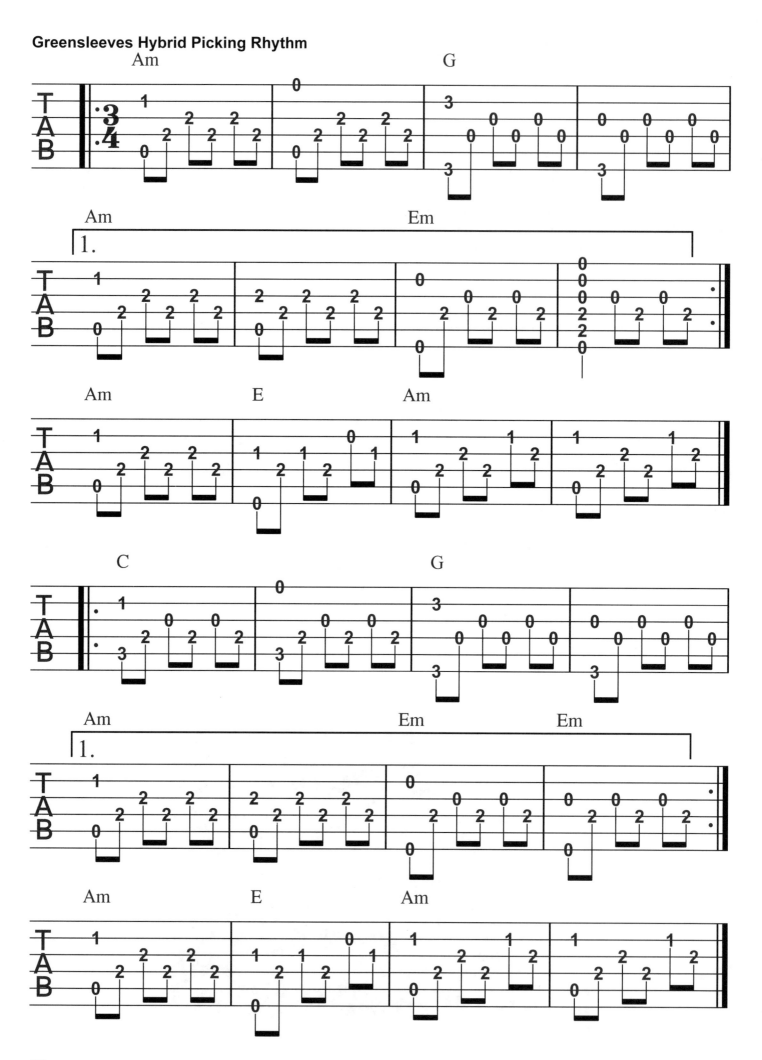

Greensleeves Melody

The Major Scale Formula

The major scale is the mother of all music. I call it this because most music starts from the major scale. The major scale is constructed using a series of whole steps and half steps. The pattern is: whole step, whole step, half step, whole step, whole step, whole step, half step, or commonly written W – W – H – W – W – W – H. If you start on any note and use this formula you will create a major scale. The starting note will also be the root note (or key). Here's an example: start with a root note C on the 5th string, 3rd fret and create a C major scale up this string.

W - C to D

W - D to E

H - E to F

W - F to G

W - G to A

W - A to B

H - B to C

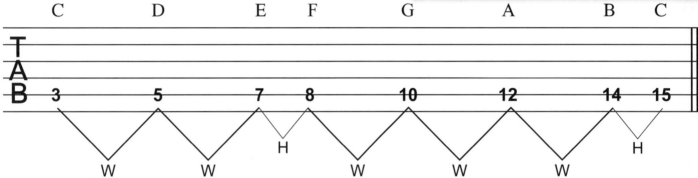

The notes that form the C major scale are C – D – E – F – G – A – B – C. This will be the only natural scale, meaning the only scale that won't need sharps or flats to make the formula work. Every other scale will have at least one sharp or flat.

MUSIC ASSIGNMENT

Once you understand how to construct major scales using the whole and half step formula use it to create major scales in a few other keys. Start with the root notes on the tab staves below and follow the sequence of whole and half steps to create major scales up each string. When constructing these scales, you'll need to add sharps to some notes to make the scale follow the formula of whole and half steps. These are called accidentals. Write the names of the notes for each scale on a piece of paper and on the tab staff below.

G   D

C Major Scale One Octave Patterns

SCALE PROFESSOR

Now that you've learned how to create a major scale using the major scale formula up one string, the next step is to take those same notes and play them in one position patterns. Below are two patterns: one starts on the 5th and one on the 6th string. Play through these two patterns:

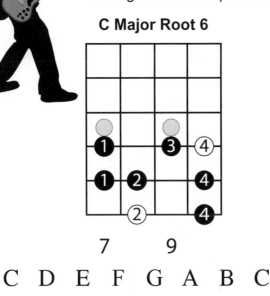

C Major Root 6

7   9

C D E F G A B C

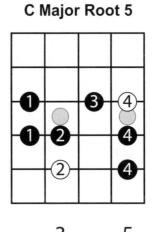

C Major Root 5

3   5

C D E F G A B C

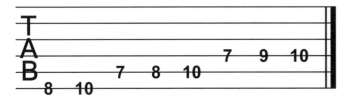

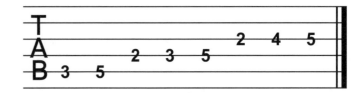

Memorize these patterns because they will be used a lot in the coming lessons. Remember that the first note is always the root note (key) and you can change the key by moving the pattern to different frets. This pattern is called a one octave pattern because it starts on the root note, and it goes up to the root note again which is eight notes higher (one octave).

MUSIC ASSIGNMENT

Now that you know the scale patterns starting on the 5th and 6th strings, lets match them up with the major open chords. Start with the A major open chord, strum the chord and then play the one octave pattern in A on the 5th and 6th string. Next, do this same exercise using the C, D, E and G open chords and corresponding scale patterns.

A   A B C♯ D E F♯ G♯ A   A B C♯ D E F♯ G♯ A

33

Major Scale Writing Assignment

Sharpen up your #2 pencil! In this lesson you will make a master list of all the sharped major scales. Using the whole/half step formula write out all seven sharped major keys C – G – D – A – E – B – F# – C#. It's important to memorize these scales because you will use them to form chords and arpeggios.

Download the sharped major scale blank work sheet to help organize the scales in key signature order. The major scale formula is: W – W – H – W – W – W – H. Accidentals (sharps or flats) will need to be added to some of the scale notes to make the whole and half steps fall between the proper steps of the scale. The following is an example of how to write these scales:

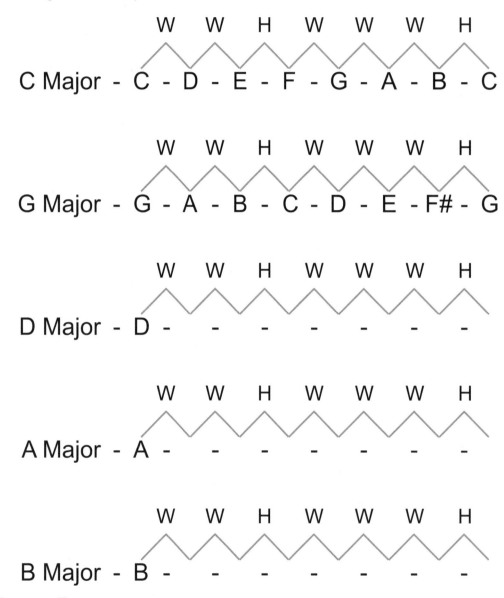

MUSIC ASSIGNMENT

After you have all seven shared major scales written out, create a saying that will help you remember the scales in key signature order. For the sharped keys the order is: G – D – A – E – B – F# – C#. One saying could be: Good – Deeds – Are – Ever – Baring – Fruit – Charley. Write your own personal saying that will help you memorize these scales.

Six String C Major Scale Patterns

CD Track
54-58

SCALE PROFESSOR

Position 1 is the root position because it starts on the C note. The C root notes are depicted in white in each of the other positions. Practice this and all scales along with a metronome using alternate picking to build up speed and accuracy.

Once you have these patterns memorized move them around the neck and play them in different keys. Your end goal is to be comfortable playing the patterns everywhere on the neck. Too often guitarists get into a comfort zone playing the patterns in only one location and when it comes time to jam with a band they get disoriented playing the patterns in fret board territory that is unfamiliar.

1st Position

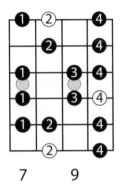

7   9

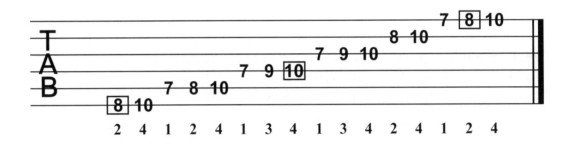

2 4 1 2 4 1 3 4 1 3 4 2 4 1 2 4

2nd Position

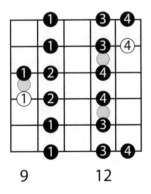

9   12

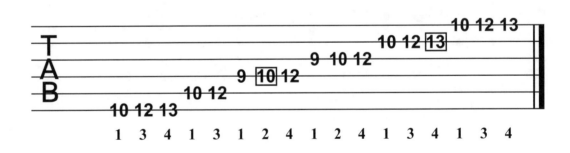

1 3 4 1 3 1 2 4 1 2 4 1 3 4 1 3 4

3rd Position

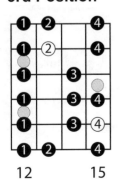

12   15

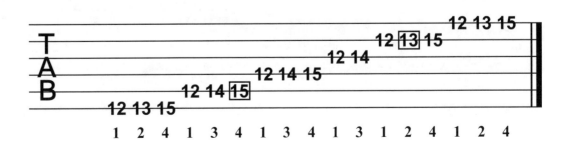

1 2 4 1 3 4 1 3 4 1 3 1 2 4 1 2 4

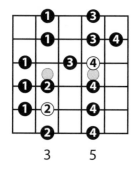
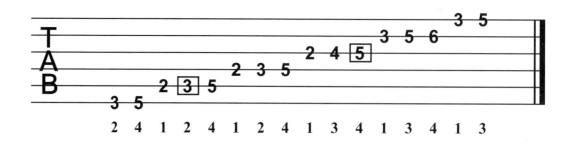

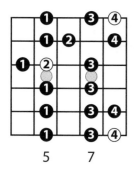
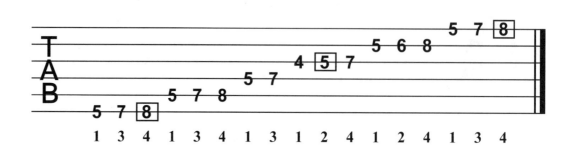

Now let's look at the C major scales across the entire neck. Below is a full neck diagram. You can see each of the five positions you learned within this diagram. Make sure to see how they connect, the second half of one is the beginning of the next. It's important to start viewing the scales on the neck as a whole as well as in the positions you learned.

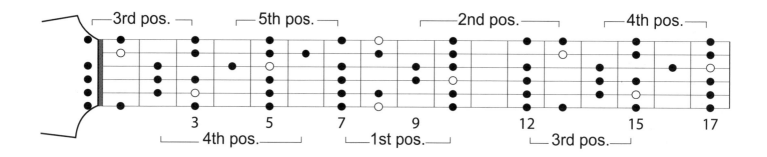

Guitar 2 Quiz #1

Once you complete this section go to RockHouseSchool.com and take the quiz to track your progress. You will receive an email with your results and suggestions.

Cannon

Here is Cannon played with a sixteenth note picking pattern. First learn the rhythm then the accompanying melody. Lastly, put the two parts together with the backing track.

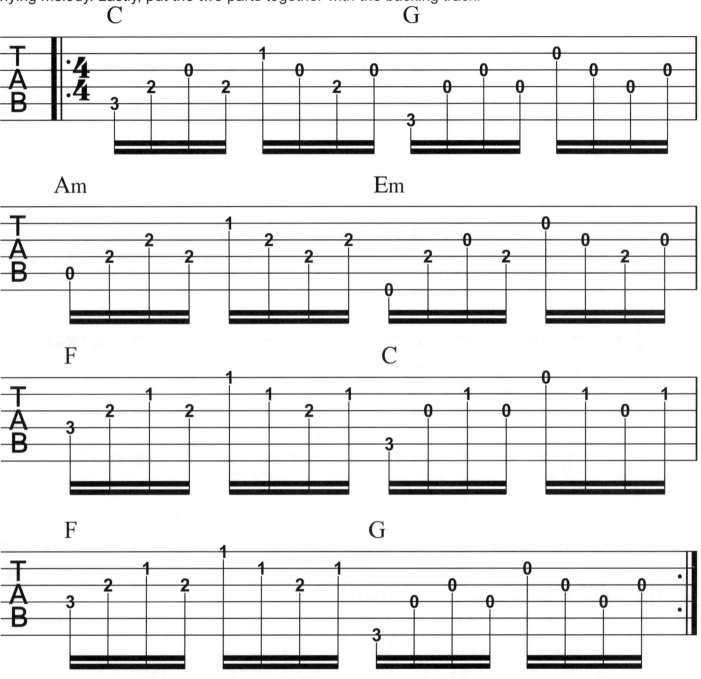

Below is the melody I created for the progression. Follow the chord names on top to keep in time with the progression. Use the full band backing track to play this melody over.

37

MUSIC ASSIGNMENT

Now lets take the Cannon rhythm and play it using a strumming pattern. The rhythm is one eighth note followed by six sixteenth notes. Make sure to follow the strum symbols below the staff.

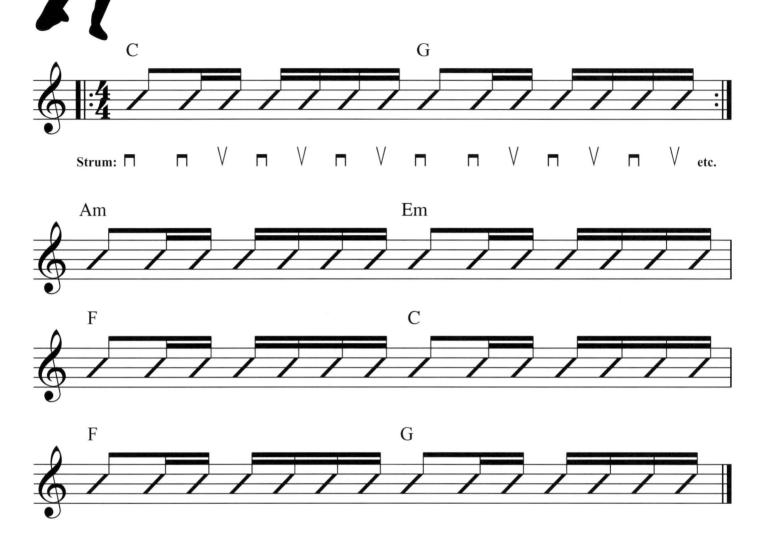

Strum: ⊓ ⊓ V ⊓ V ⊓ V ⊓ ⊓ V ⊓ V ⊓ V etc.

The Mexican Snake Song

C Major 1 - 4 - 5 Progression

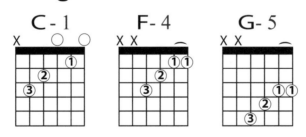

38

Major Scale Triplet Lead Pattern

Here is the 1st position C major scale played in triplets. Lead patterns are a great way to experience new phrasings while playing the scales. Think of the scales as your alphabet. Practicing lead patterns is similar to improving your writing or typing skills. The more control you have over scale patterns, the easier it will be to play creative and interesting melodies. Practice along with a metronome and keep the timing even and steady. Count "one trip-let, two trip-let" out loud to get familiar with the triplet timing.

1st Position

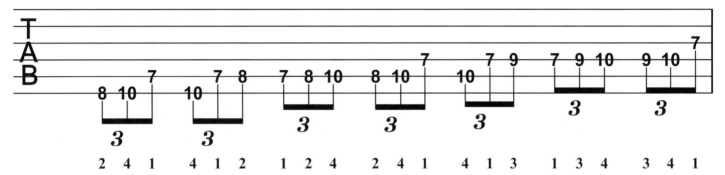

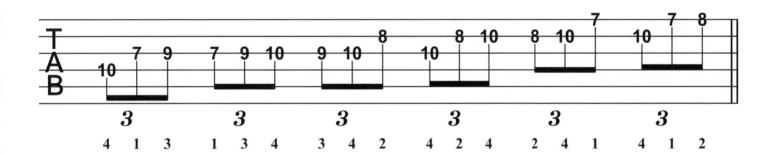

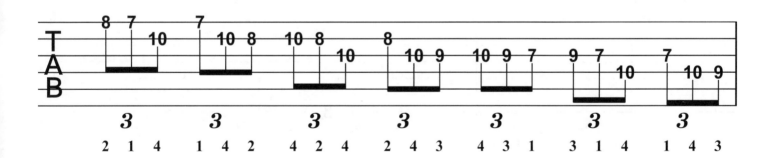

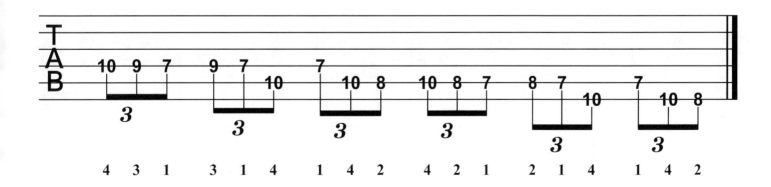

Exercise Workout Routine

The following workout section contains a series of exclusive Rock House finger exercises designed to strengthen specific areas of your playing technique. All of these exercises should be practiced along with a metronome. Start out slowly and build speed gradually using proper technique.

The Killer

Use consistent alternate picking throughout. Play through the first measure slowly until you memorize the pattern. For each consecutive measure, the pattern moves down one string. The third tab staff shows the pattern in reverse.

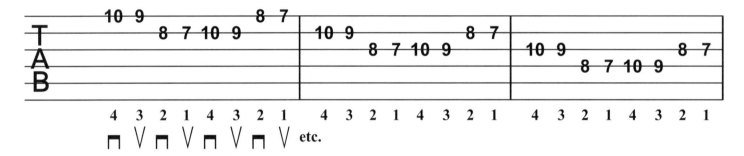

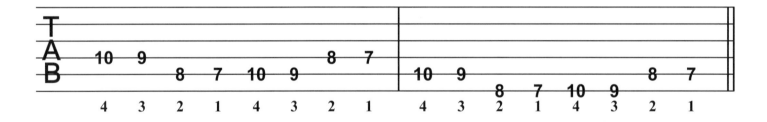

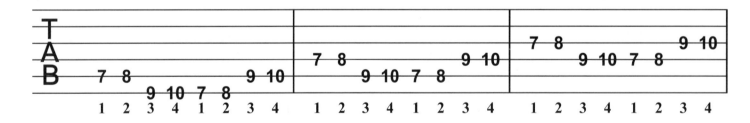

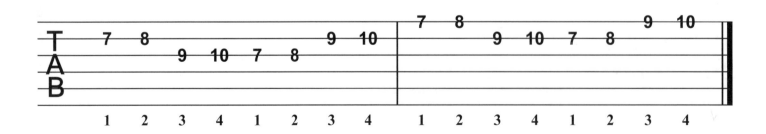

Hammer Rolls

This exercise will help to strengthen the hammer on and pull off techniques. The fingering and fret numbers are the same on each string, and the pattern moves up in groups of three strings for each measure. Play each group of three notes using a smooth triplet feel, picking the first note and hammering on for the next two notes. The second tab staff shows the example in reverse, this time using pull offs and moving down in groups of three strings.

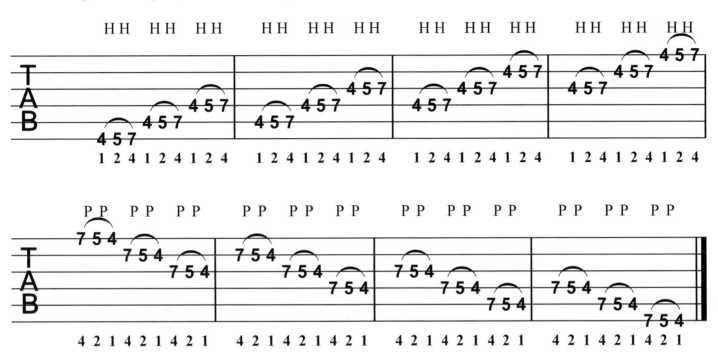

One Hand Rolls

Here's an exercise designed to strengthen your left hand using a series of hammer ons and pull offs. Pick the very first note of the exercise, then all of the notes should be sounded by the left hand only; don't use the pick at all for the rest of the notes. Your right hand should be used to mute the other strings.

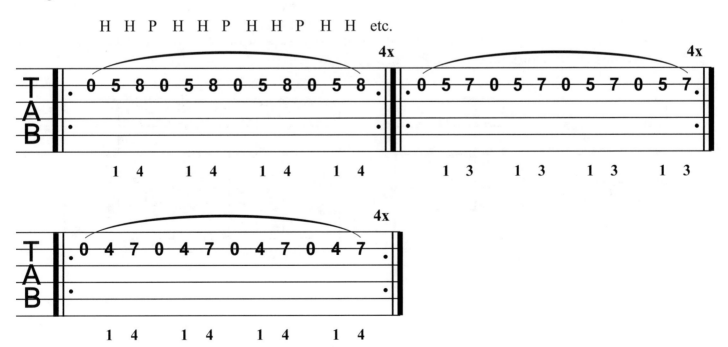

Finger Crusher

Each section of this exercise starts with a two string pattern taken from the A minor pentatonic scale. Play it four times in position, then move the pattern chromatically (one fret at a time) up the neck to the 12th fret and chromatically back down to where you started at the 5th fret. Keep time with the metronome and make it your goal to get through the entire exercise without stopping.

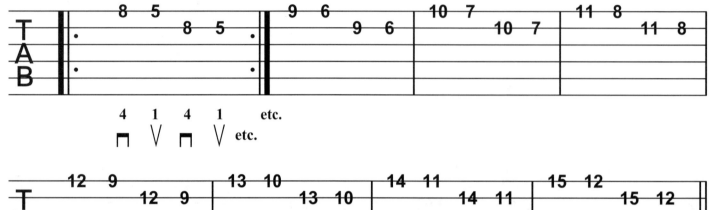

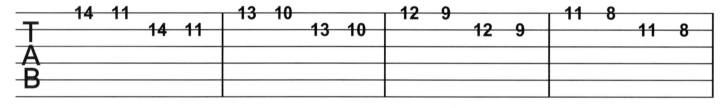

Below are the four remaining two string groupings from the first position minor pentatonic scale. Apply the pattern above to play through each of these groupings.

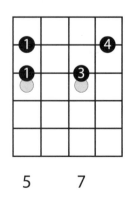

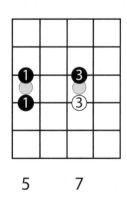

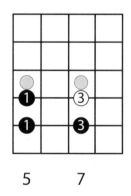

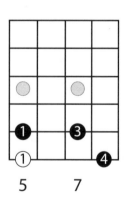

Chord Formulas & Construction

Now that you understand the major scale, it's time to learn how chords are formed. By isolating certain scale degrees and playing them together you form chords. I'll start with major and minor chord formulas from the root C to give you an example of how this works. First, look below at the full major scale with the corresponding scale degree numbers:

C Major Scale: C - D - E - F - G - A - B - C

 1 - 2 - 3 - 4 - 5 - 6 - 7 - 8

Major Chords

To form a major chord you take the 1st, 3rd and 5th degrees of the major scale. So from the root C the three notes would be C – E – G.

C Major: C - E - G
Major Chord Formula: 1 - 3 - 5

Minor Chords

To form a minor chord you take the same three notes but flat the 3rd degree of the major scale. The three notes of a C minor chord would be C – Eb – G. Play these three notes anywhere on the guitar neck to form a C minor chord.

C Minor: C - E$^\flat$ - G
Minor Chord Formula: 1 - $^\flat$3 - 5

A major chord has a major 3rd interval from the 1st to the 3rd degree, this is two whole steps. A minor chord has a minor interval from the 1st to the 3rd degree, this is a whole and half step or a step and a half. Take notice of the intervals that create a major and minor chord because this will help you understand music better. On the next page are some chords with the intervals outlined under each string. Pick each string and hear what the intervals sound like.

MUSIC ASSIGNMENT

There are many ways to combine the notes of a chord to make new fingerings across the neck. Many guitarists create there own chord variations to get unique sounds. A great way to see all the notes across the neck used to form a chord is to write them out on a neck diagram. Below see the neck diagram for the C major chord notes C – E – G. This is every note across the neck that can be used to play a C major chord. Combine these notes together and form your own C major chords. Write your chords out on blank chord paper so you can use them to create your own songs. Using blank full neck diagram sheets from the *Lesson Support* site write out all the notes up each string for the G (G – B – D) and D minor (D – F – A) chords.

C Major Chord Tones

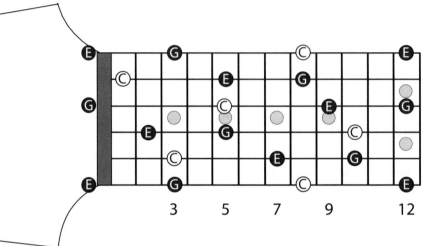

Minor Bar Chords

CHORD PROFESSOR

Minor bar chords are similar to the major bar chords. Like the major bar chords these are movable and can be played on any fret across the neck. Play the two minor chord forms below. These chords will move up the neck and follow the same name chart as the major forms. For example, if you play the F minor form on the 5th fret it would be an A minor chord, and if you play the Bb minor form at the 5th fret it would be a D minor chord. The root (chord name) is found on the 6th and 5th strings.

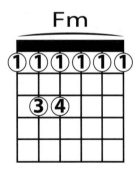

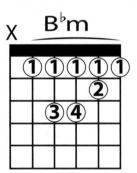

Name -	F	F#	G	G#	A	A#	B	C	C#	D	D#	E
Fret -	1	2	3	4	5	6	7	8	9	10	11	12
Name -	Bb	B	C	C#	D	D#	E	F	F#	G	G#	A

Voodoo Girl
6 - 2 - 1 - 5 Progression

This 6 - 2 - 1 - 5 progression combines major and minor bar chords. I refer to this progression as a "square progression" because of the way the chords go from one to another in a square type pattern. Pay attention to the strum pattern below the staff.

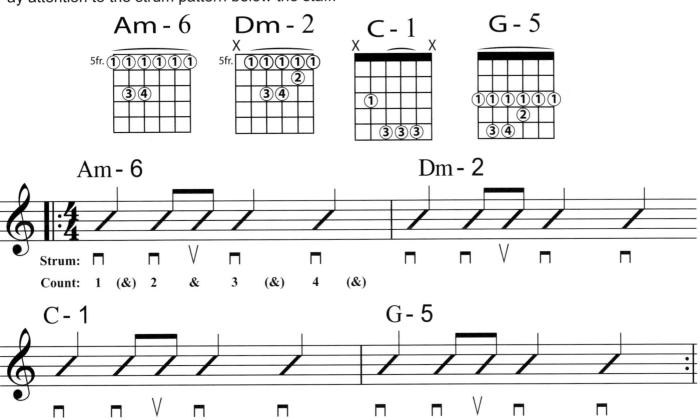

Arpeggios

Arpeggios are formed by taking the notes of a chord and picking them separately, not letting any notes ring together. An A major arpeggio is formed using the notes A – C# – E which are the 1st, 3rd and 5th degrees of the A major scale. These are also the notes of an A major chord. An A minor arpeggio is formed using the notes A – C – E, these are also the notes of an A minor chord with the 3rd flatted. Take the notes of any chord, play them consecutively in any order and you are playing an arpeggio.

Major Arpeggio

Example 1

The following examples are two octave A major arpeggios. Follow the picking symbols and use consistent alternate picking:

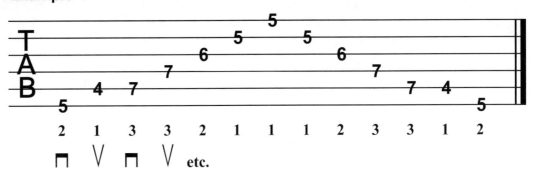

Example 2

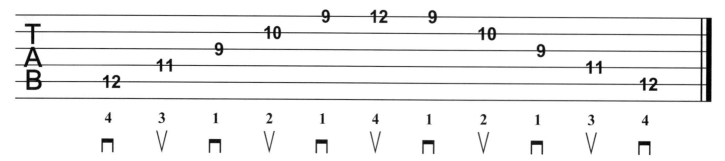

Minor Arpeggio

The following examples are two octave A minor arpeggios. Follow the picking symbols and use consistent alternate picking.

Example 1

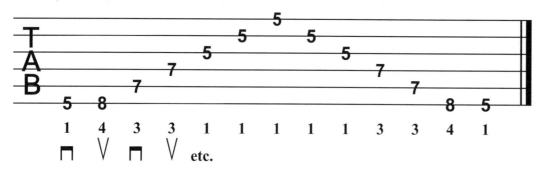

Example 2

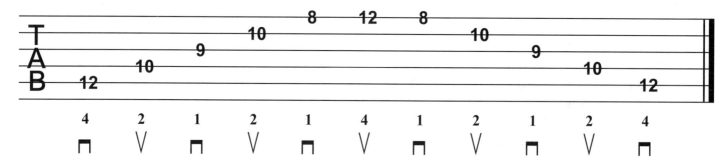

Notice there is only a small difference between the major and minor arpeggios. All of the 3rds in the minor arpeggios are one fret (or one half step) lower than the 3rds in the major arpeggio. This slight difference is what makes a chord or an arpeggio either major or minor. These notes are also referred to as major 3rds or minor 3rds.

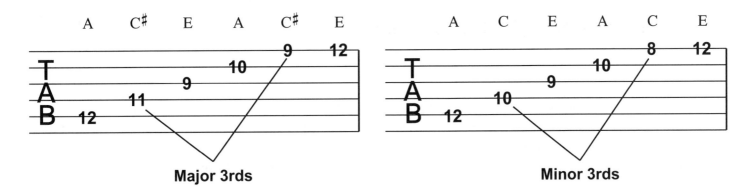

Major 3rds

Minor 3rds

The notes of an arpeggio can be stacked and played anywhere on the neck. Just like scales, you can map the notes of any arpeggio across the fret board to see all the possible variations. These are called "arpeggio patterns." Below is an A major and an A minor full neck arpeggio pattern. Play any combination of these notes to create your own arpeggios. Make sure to write any arpeggios you create in tablature to use in the future.

A Major

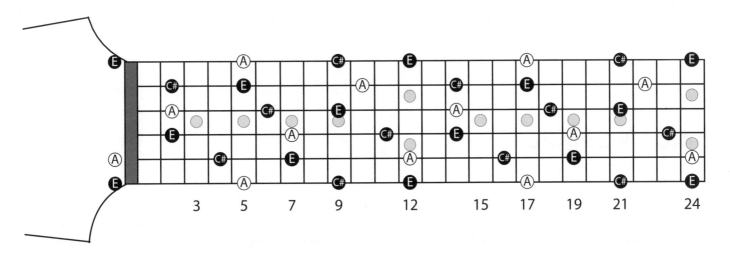

A Minor

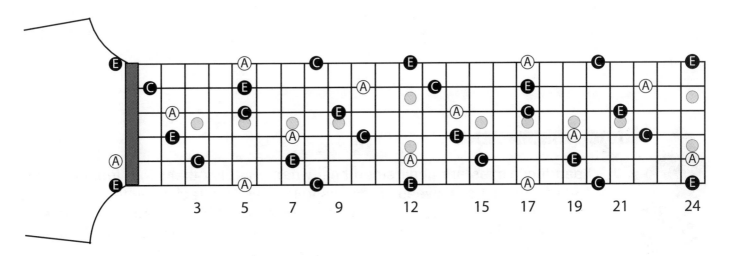

Sweep Picking Exercise

Sweep picking is performed by dragging the pick across the strings in one smooth, flowing motion up or down. In the example below, sweep downward with the pick to the first string, hammer pull off and then sweep upward to the 6th string. Don't peck at the strings, keep your hand locked as you drag it across the strings. Sweep picking is a very useful technique for playing fast arpeggio runs.

Major Arpeggio

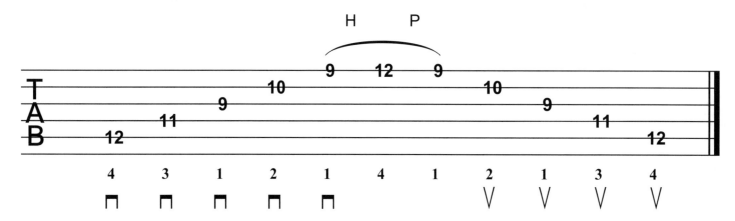

Minor Arpeggio

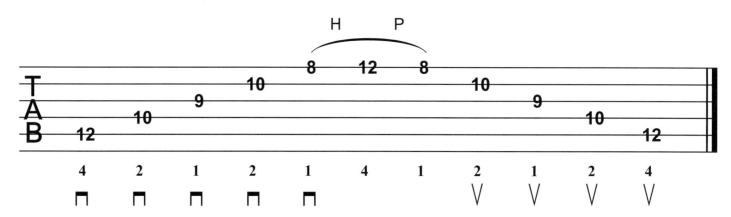

MUSIC ASSIGNMENT

Lead techniques are understood best when you play them with feel in a band setting. Apply these sweep arpeggios to the backing tracks and then add in the other elements to craft some leads and melodies. Tab out your ideas and start your own "licktionary," per se. The ideas you write down will be your own unique licks and riffs that will define you as a lead player on a whole new level.

Single Note Riffs

Single note riffs are used in song writing by guitarists in all genres of music. Often times the single note riff becomes a hook in the song. From the "Beatles" to "Ozzy" there has been hit song after hit song written using single note riffs. Here are a few single note riffs so you can see how they are constructed and understand how they fit into a songs structure. The following riffs are in the key of "E" minor.

Riff #1

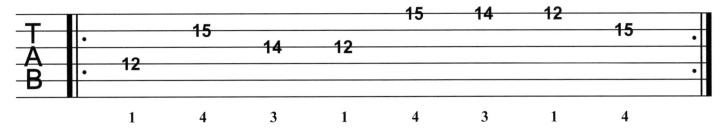

Riff #2

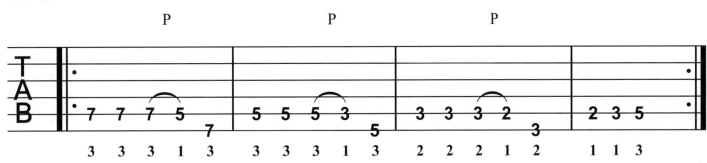

Riff #3

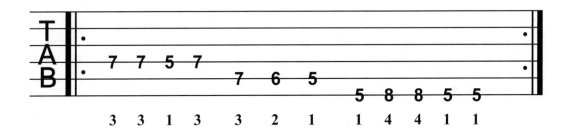

MUSIC ASSIGNMENT

Single note riffs are often created right from scales. If a song is in the key "A" minor you would use the A minor scale to create a single note riff. Use the A minor scale and create your own single note riffs. Remember that the root note should be a strong tone within the riff. Write all riffs out in tablature. Have some fun being creative!

Syncopation
Accenting the Up Beat

By definition, syncopation is an accent on a normally unaccented beat. Syncopation often occurs on the upbeat because a normal music feel would be everything on a down beat. When you start hitting notes on an up beat, it's more unexpected, and it creates syncopation. To better understand this feel strum the D major open chord in up accents. Count out loud as you play to hear and feel the rhythm. The strums are all hit where the "&" falls within the count. Mute the chord after each strum making it cut short and not ring. So you strum up and then mute the chord by letting the pressure off the chord immediately after you strike it choking the sound. Certain genres of music such as reggae and ska focus heavily on accenting the upbeat in this manner.

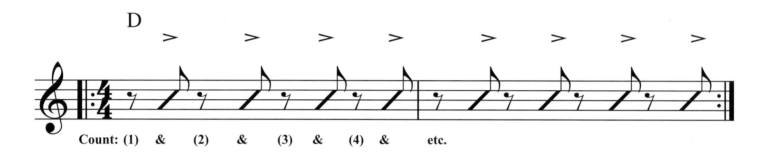

Yeah Mon
Reggae 1 - 4 - 5 Progression

CD Track71-72

Grab your bathing suit and sun block because you're going to learn a genre of music that is usually associated with the Caribbean Islands: reggae. Strum the chords only up and use the muted or choked technique after strumming each chord. Move your body and sway to the music. It's important to get your body clock into the rhythm of the music.

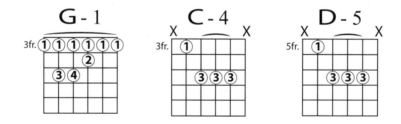

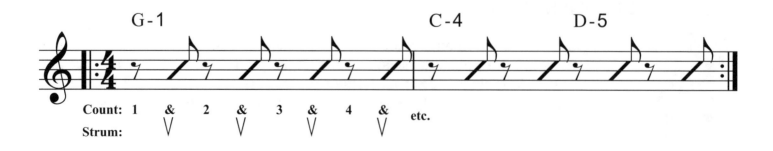

Natural Minor Scales

SCALE PROFESSOR

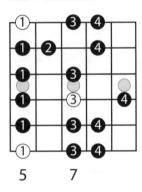

The natural minor scale is a seven note scale. It is the pure minor scale also known as the Aeolian mode. In this lesson you will learn all five scale positions in the key of "A." The notes of the A natural minor scale are A – B – C – D – E – F – G. This scale sounds a bit more melodic then the pentatonic scale, this is because the intervals are smaller between notes. The root notes or A notes are in white. Memorize the finger patterns on each string to help you learn these scales.

1st Position

5   7

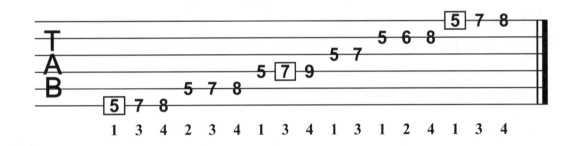

1 3 4 2 3 4 1 3 4 1 3 1 2 4 1 3 4

2nd Position

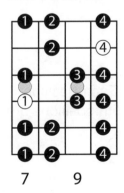

7   9

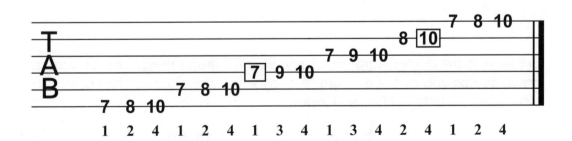

1 2 4 1 2 4 1 3 4 1 3 4 2 4 1 2 4

3rd Position

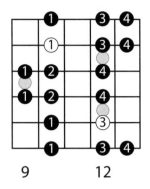

9   12

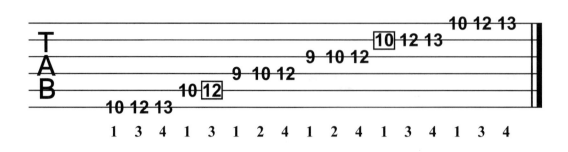

1 3 4 1 3 1 2 4 1 2 4 1 3 4 1 3 4

4th Position

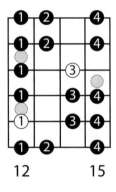

12   15

This scale position can be played one octave (12 frets) lower. Play this scale starting on the open 6th string.

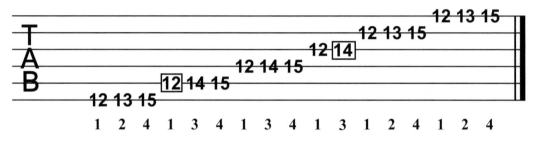

1 2 4 1 3 4 1 3 4 1 3 1 2 4 1 2 4

5th Position

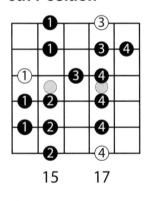

15   17

This scale position can be played one octave (12 frets) lower. Play this scale starting on the 6th string 3rd fret.

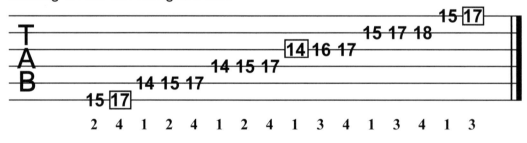

2 4 1 2 4 1 2 4 1 3 4 1 3 4 1 3

Below is a full neck diagram that shows the natural minor scales across the neck. Each position is bracketed so you can see where they lay within the diagram. Notice how the 4th and 5th positions are also found an octave (12 frets) lower.

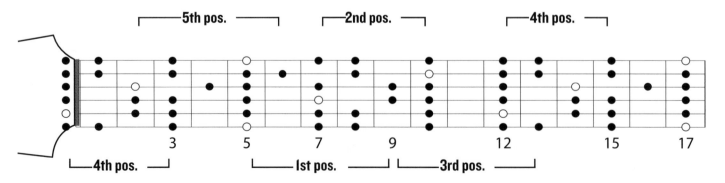

The following diagram shows you how each scale connects to the next position. The second half of each scale is the first half of the next. Play through each scale and see how they connect.

Connecting the Five Positions

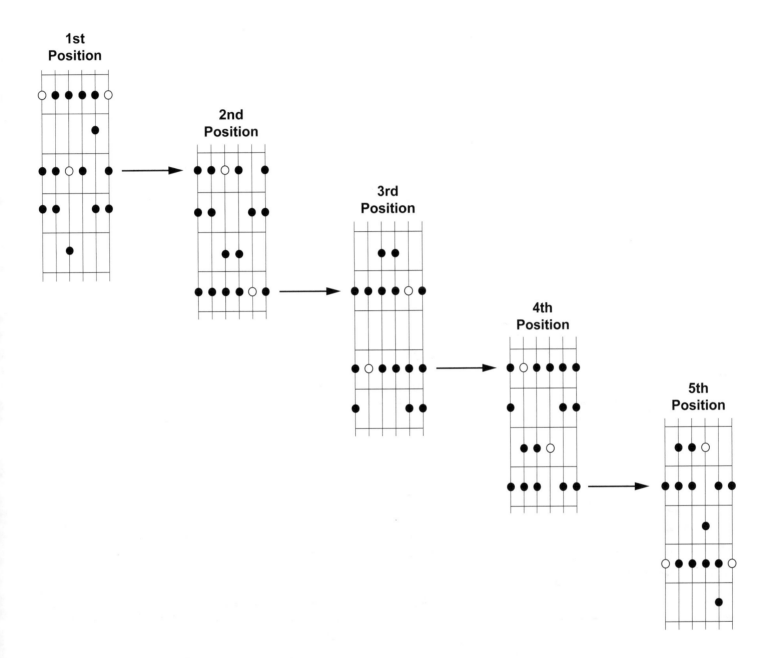

Guitar 2 Quiz #2

Once you complete this section go to RockHouseSchool.com and take the quiz to track your progress. You will receive an email with your results and suggestions.

Natural Minor Scale Lead Pattern

Now that you have learned the natural minor scale patterns lets put them into an interesting pattern. This is a triplet pattern played from each scale degree. By varying the scale notes into patterns you clearly see how they transform into leads. Use alternate picking and build your speed up gradually.

1st Position

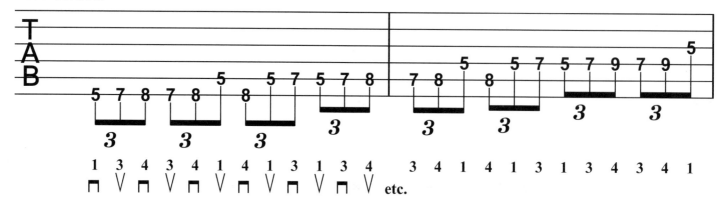

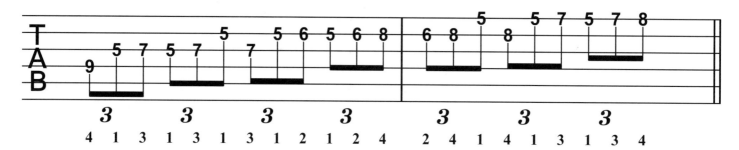

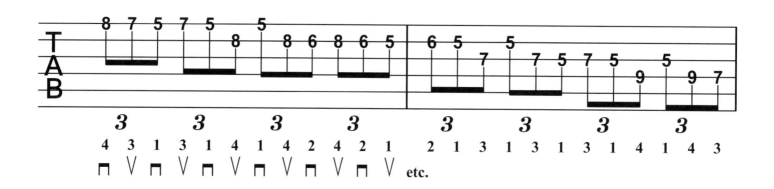

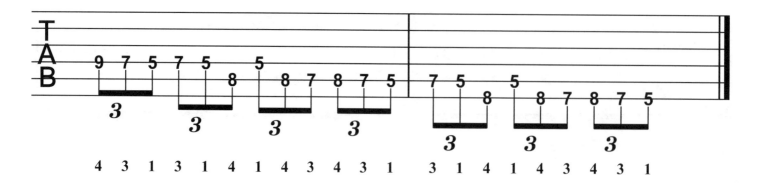

Hooked on Blues
Sliding Note Blues

This riff uses the slide technique to create a blues sound. The riff combines rhythm and lead together which is a common blues technique.

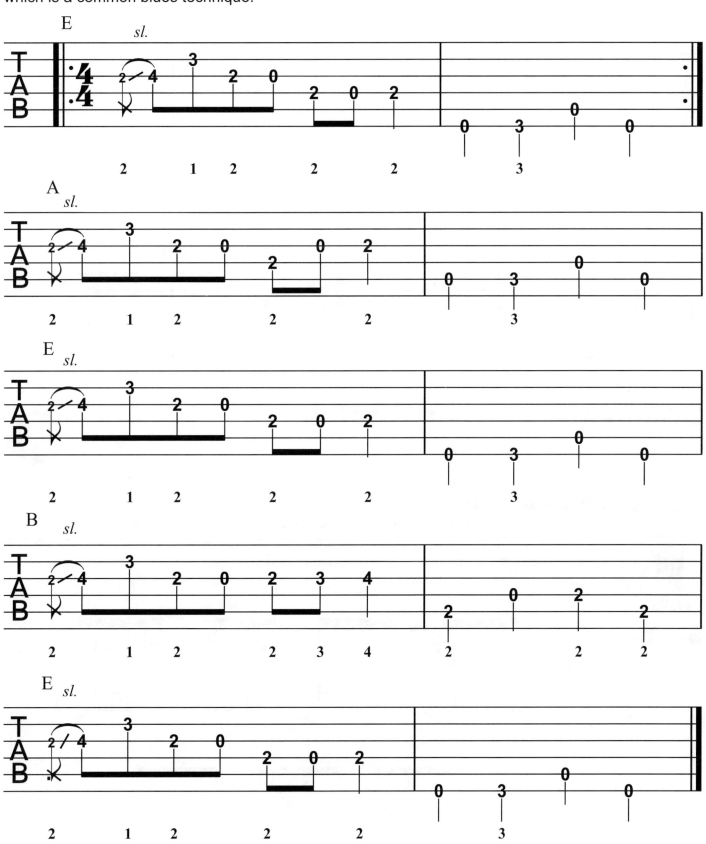

Octaves

Octaves are a common intervallic technique used in lead and rhythm guitar applications. There are a few shapes that are most characteristic that incorporate a string skip. Although you strum three strings you only sound two while deadening the string in the middle with the back of your first finger. Many players use octaves to enhance a melody line making it stand out in a song. Play through the following octave shapes and move them around the neck to different frets.

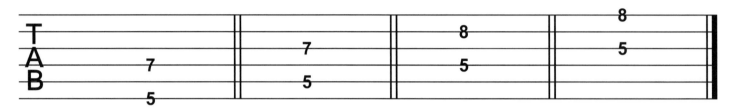

You can use octaves to help you memorize the names of the notes on the guitar. There is a connection between the 6th, 4th, and 2nd strings and the 5th, 3rd and 1st strings. See the tab below how this works:

Dominant 7th Open Chords

CHORD PROFESSOR

Dominant seventh chords are similar to major chords only with an added flat 7 note (we'll get into the theory of chord formulas later in this book). This chord's unique sound creates tension and is often used in blues music.

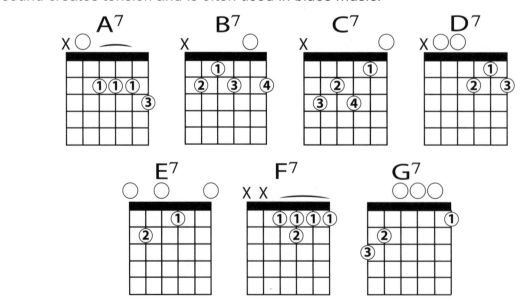

7th Heaven
1 - 4 - 5 Progression

Dominant seventh chords are commonly substituted for the chords in a 1 – 4 – 5 chord progression. This gives the progression a very bluesy sound. Below is a 1 – 4 – 5 progression using dominant seventh chords in the key of "A." The strum pattern is: down – down up – up down up. Play this progression over the bass and drum backing track.

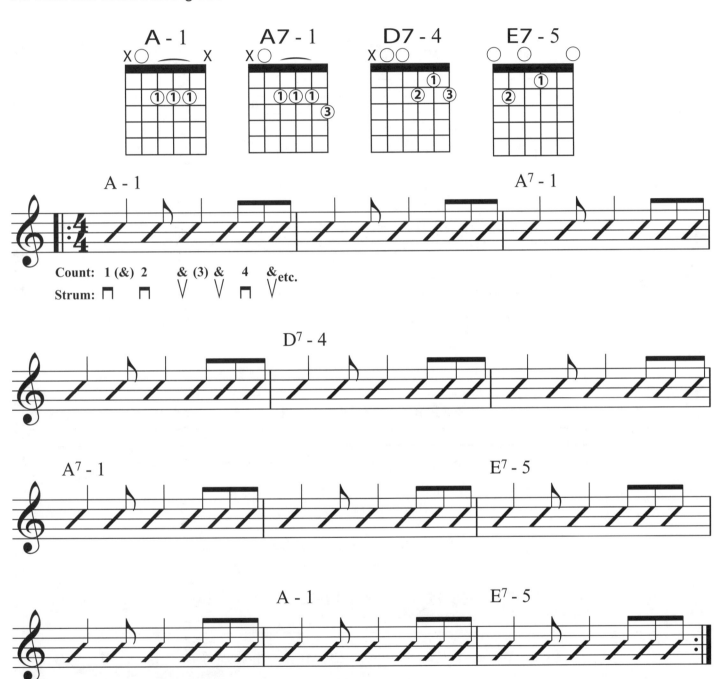

MUSIC ASSIGNMENT

Create several different I – IV – V chord progressions using your open dominant seventh chords. Here are a few to start with. E7th – A7th – B7th and G7th – C7th – D7th. Try different strum patterns and be creative.

Pentatonic Lateral Runs

By learning the minor pentatonic scale positions up one string at a time you see the scales in a new perspective. It's time to take these scales and lay them out in this fashion so you can move to the next level. Below I have given you an example of playing the A minor pentatonic scale up all six strings. Play through these and really take notice of how the notes come from the five positions you already know.

1st String

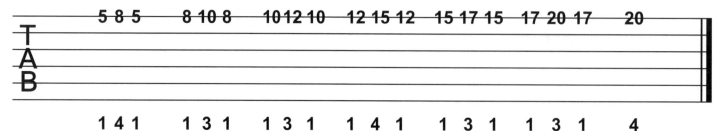

2nd String

3rd String

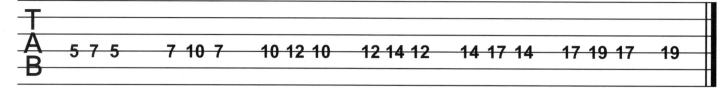

4th String

5th String

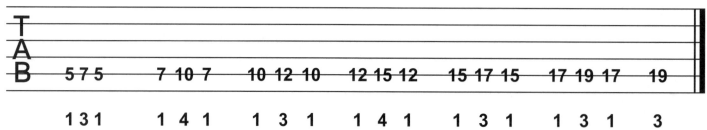

6th String

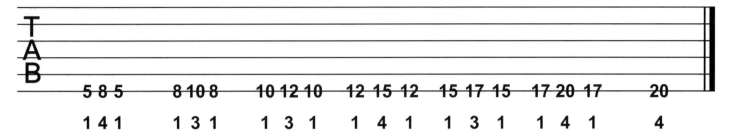

5 8 5   8 10 8   10 12 10   12 15 12   15 17 15   17 20 17   20

1 4 1   1 3 1   1 3 1   1 4 1   1 3 1   1 4 1   4

Riff Challenge #2

CD Track
83-85

Here are another group of riffs to rip into. Have fun, start slow and build up speed gradually.

Riff #1 E minor

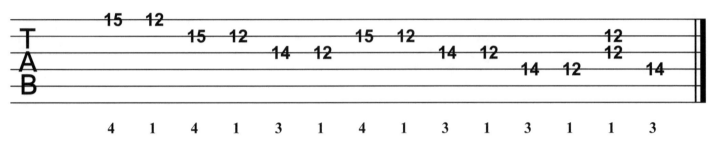

4   1   4   1   3   1   4   1   3   1   3   1   1   3

Riff #2 A minor

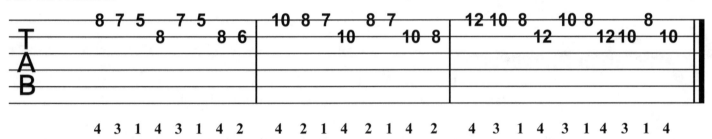

4 3 1 4 3 1 4 2   4 2 1 4 2 1 4 2   4 3 1 4 3 1 4 3 1 4

Riff #3 E minor

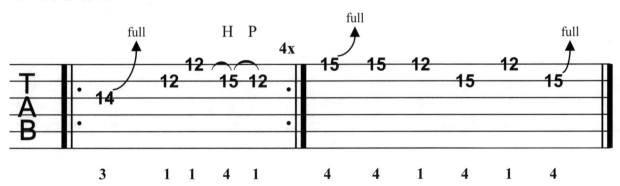

3   1 1 4 1   4   4   1   4   1   4

Drop D Tuning

In Drop D tuning the 6th string is lowered one whole step while the other five strings stay at standard pitch. From low to high the strings would be tuned as follows D – A – D – G – B – E.

To tune in drop D pick the open 4th string D and let it ring out, then pick your 6th string open and tune it down slowly until you hear the D pitches come together. Now you are in drop D tuning. In the next lessons you will play chords and rhythms in drop D.

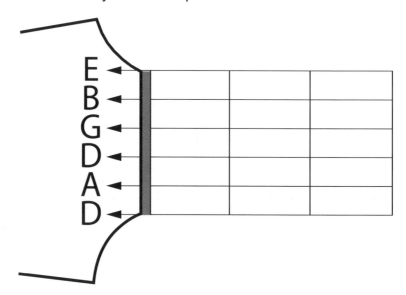

Drop D Tuning Chords

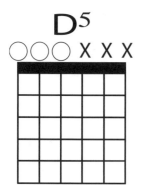 ## Chord Professor

Once your guitar is tuned to drop D tuning there will be chord fingerings that will work more effectively and new inversions that will be born. The biggest asset in this tuning is the ability to play full power chords by just barring the fattest three strings. Because the low string is now a D note many bands using this tuning write songs in the key of "D" to take advantage of the heavy open string sound. Below see some common chords used in this tuning:

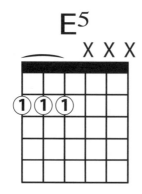

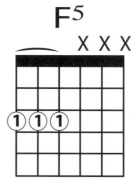

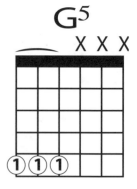

Mean Street
Drop D Rhythm

CD Track
87-88

Play this rhythm along with the bass and drum backing track and get comfortable with the syncopated chord change. Mute the strings to get different dynamic sounds. After you've mastered this rhythm, experiment and create your own rhythms and riffs in drop D tuning.

$D^5 \quad F^5 \quad G^5 \qquad\qquad\qquad D^5$

```
T |.                                        .|| .                              . |
A |                                          || .                                |
B |. 0 0    3 3   5 5                 .|| . 0 0 0 0 0 0 0 0 .|
  |  0 0    3 3   5 5            5    ||   0 0 0 0 0 0 0 0   |
  |  0 0    3 3   5 5   0 5 6  6     ||   0 0 0 0 0 0 0 0   |
```

3x

MUSIC ASSIGNMENT

With your guitar in standard E tuning, improvise over the backing track using D minor pentatonic scales. Below are the five D minor pentatonic scales. Start by just playing them forward and backwards. Next use the bending and hammer pull off techniques within these scales to create your own lead.

D Minor Pentatonic Scale

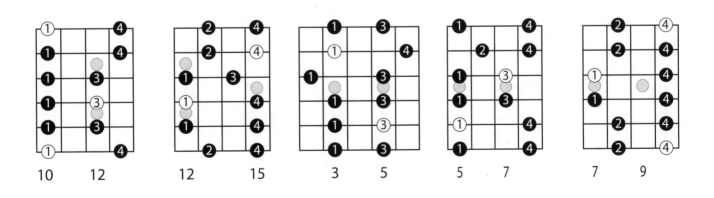

Multi Position Lead Patterns

Lead patterns don't have to stay within one scale position. Many times when a guitarist is creating a lead they move laterally across the neck. Here are a few multi position lead patterns that will help you connect your scales across the neck:

Minor Pentatonic Two Position Follow Pattern
Ascending

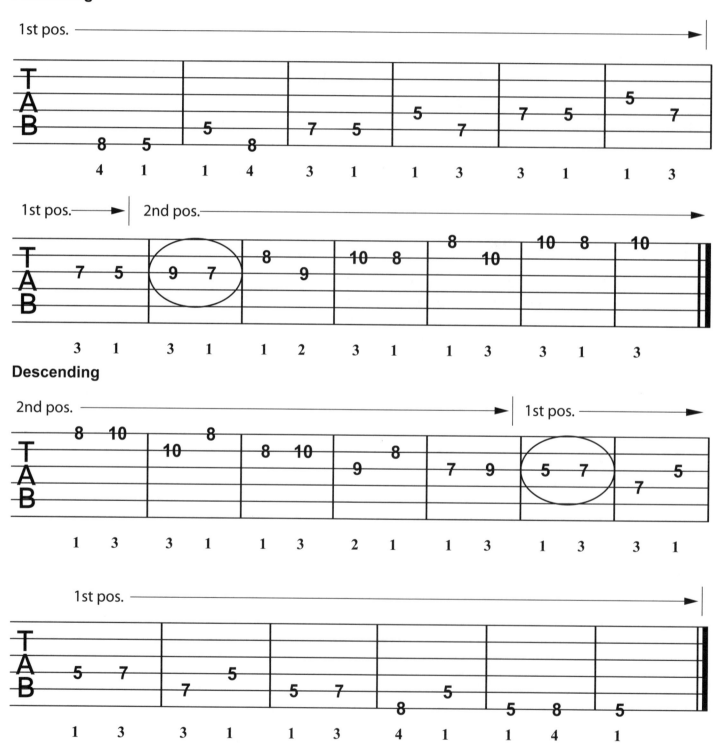

Descending

Minor Pentatonic Two Position Triplet Pattern
Ascending

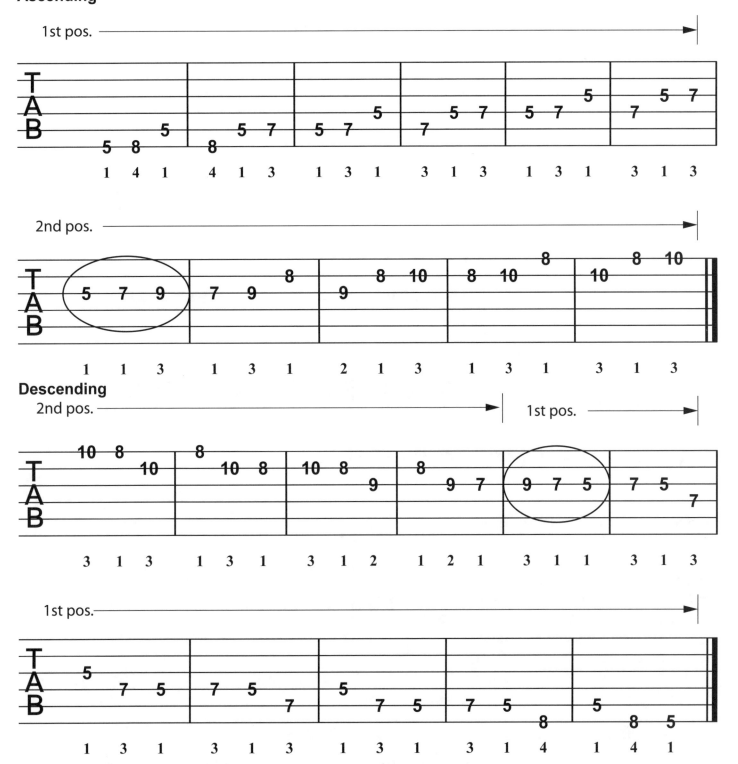

Descending

Modes Demystified

Modes are subdivisions of the major scale that create unique sounds. The Rock House Method offers a unique learning system for learning and applying the modes called "Modes Demystified." At this point you are ready to begin working with "Modes Demystified" as a supplement to your current studies.

Major & Minor 7th Full Form Chords

CHORD PROFESSOR

Now let's learn major 7th (M7) and minor 7th (m7) full form chords. These chords have no open strings so they are all moveable. The 7th chords are extensions of the original major and minor chords which add a new note giving it more flavor and a jazzier sound.

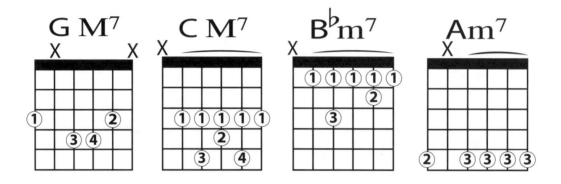

The ii – V – I Progression

CD Track
91-92

Another common chord progression is the 2 – 5 – 1 progression (also written ii – V – I). In this progression chords are built from the 2nd, 5th and 1st degrees of a major scale. You will use M7 and m7 chords from the previous lesson plus a new dominant 7th chord fingering. This

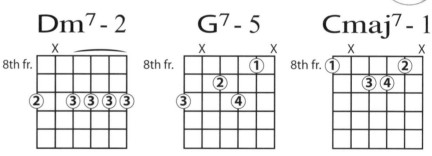

progression is most popular in jazz music but can be found in many other genres. The progression in the lesson is in the key of "C."

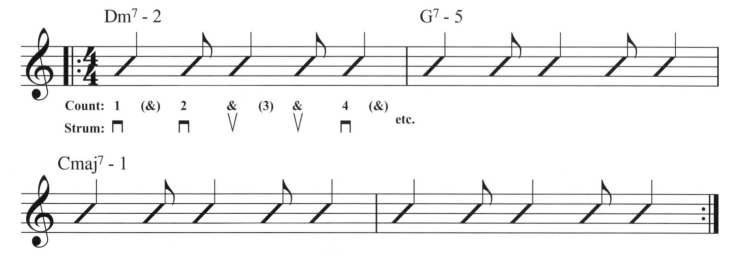

ii – V – I Lead Patterns

Let's learn a pattern to play over the ii – V – I progression. The pattern in this lesson follows the notes of each chord played separately. You can hear the sound of each chord by just playing the lead pattern because they outline the chord tones. Many jazz players use patterns that follow the chord tones. Pay attention to the chord changes above the tablature staff to see the connection.

Pattern 1

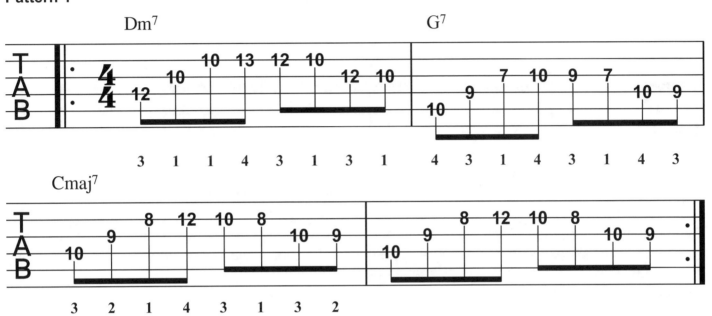

Pattern 2

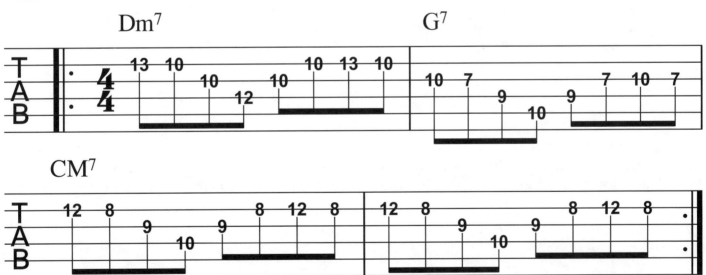

CAGED Sequence Basic Shapes

The CAGED system is a useful method to help you visualize the fret board. There are literally thousands of different species of chords and chord shapes that can be played on the guitar, most can be traced back to just five common open forms. The five forms are C, A, G, E, and D that spells CAGED and that's how this system got its name. By knowing the relationship of each chord shape to the next across the neck you will begin to see the neck as a whole instead of a bunch of little sections. You already know these five chord shapes from the open major chords so let's look at these first.

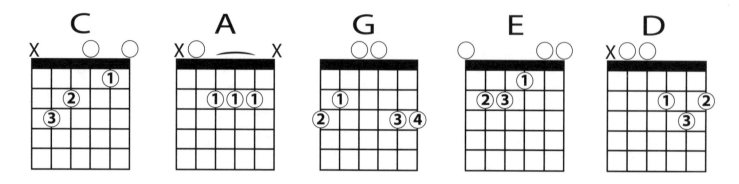

If you take the three notes of any major chord and map a full neck diagram across the neck you will see these five chord shapes within that diagram. Below is a fret board diagram of the C major chord tones C – E – G. I've isolated the five chords shapes within it so you can see where they are found and how they connect to each other.

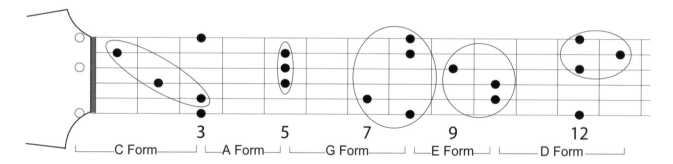

Now let's make a fret board diagram for the E major scale tones E – G# – B. As you can see below, all five shapes are still found within this diagram. Even though the first chord is E it still follows the same order just starting with E and going E – D – C – A – G then it would loop back to E in a circle fashion.

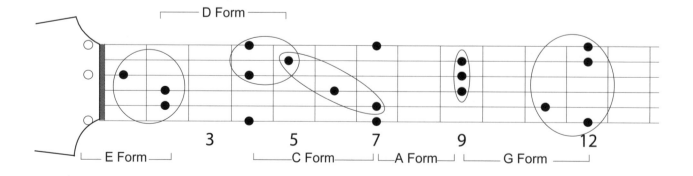

With a little practice with the CAGED system you will be able to find any major chord easily anywhere on the neck.

 **MUSIC ASSIGNMENT**

Here is an exercise to apply the caged system across the neck. I will show you the five closed form caged system chords for the key of "C" and "E" along with the full neck diagram for each. Keep in mind that these are all C and E major chords even though they are the five CAGED shapes. As you play these chords up the neck visualize the chord before and after each so you see the connection between them all.

C Major Chords

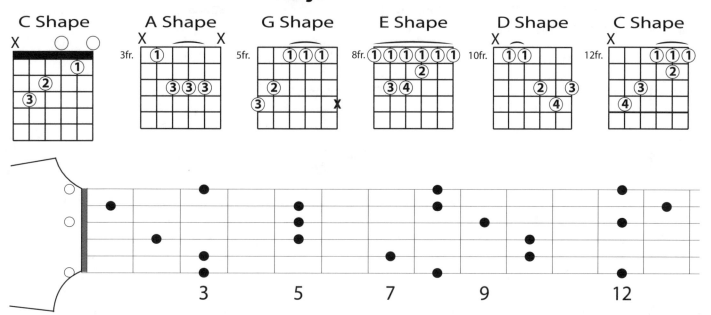

E Major Chords

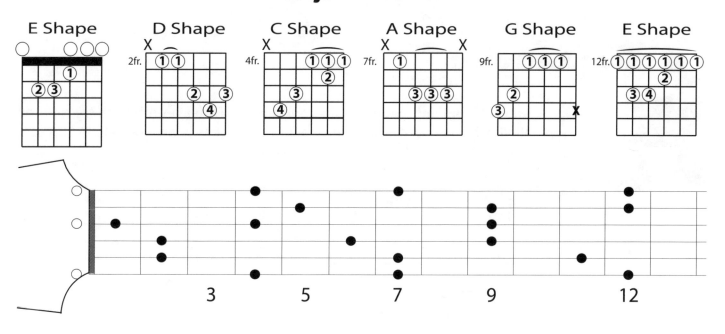

Bi-Dextral Hammer On's

This right hand tapping technique is executed by tapping notes on the neck with your picking hand. Hammer the right hand finger down, then pull off to sound another note fretted with your left hand. This technique allows you to hammer and pull off full arpeggios and other wide interval phrases very quickly creating a unique sound. The "T" above the tab staff indicates a right hand tap. Right hand tapping was made popular by Eddie Van Halen, who incorporated tapping in many of his famous solos.

```
    T P  H   T P  H   T P  H   T P  H            T P  H    T P  H    T P  H    T P  H

T ‖|• 9 2 5 9 2 5 9 2 5 9 2 5 •‖|• 10 2 5 10 2 5 10 2 5 10 2 5 •‖
A |•                          •|•                                •|
B |•                          •|•                                •|

    ①  1  4 ① 1  4 ① 1  4 ① 1  4      ①  1  4 ①  1  4 ①  1  4 ①  1  4
```

```
    T P  H   T P  H   T P  H   T P  H            T P  H    T P  H    T P  H    T P  H

T ‖|• 10 4 7 10 4 7 10 4 7 10 4 7 •‖|• 12 4 7 12 4 7 12 4 7 12 4 7 •‖
A |•                              •|•                                •|
B |•                              •|•                                •|

    ①  1  4 ① 1  4 ① 1  4 ① 1  4      ①  1  4 ①  1  4 ①  1  4 ①  1  4
```

MUSIC ASSIGNMENT

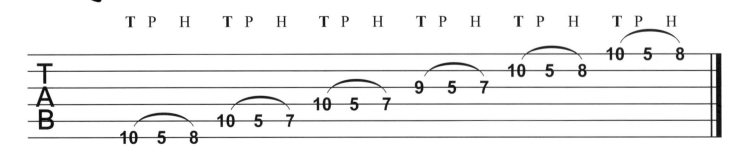

Experiment with tapping notes within your scales. Don't be afraid to try different combinations; this is how great ideas are formed. Below is an example to kick start the process using the first two minor pentatonic scales in the key of "A."

```
    T P   H   T P   H    T P   H    T P   H    T P   H    T P   H

T                                                             10  5  8
A                                              9  5  7   10  5  8
B             10  5  7   10  5  7
   10  5  8
```

68

Guitar 2 Quiz #3

Congratulations you've made it to the end of Book 2! Go to RockHouseSchool.com and take the quiz to track your progress. You will receive an email with your results and an official Rock House Method "Certificate of Completion" when you pass.

Musical Words

Progression: A series of chords that are played within a song.

Accent: A louder pick or strum.

Dynamics: The variation of sound levels, louder and softer.

Riff: A short melody usually 2 or 4 beats long.

5th Position: The section of the guitar spanning the 5th through 8th frets across all six strings.

Triplet: A group of three notes played in the time of two of the same notes.

Natural Minor Scale: The natural minor scale has the same tones as the major scale, but uses the sixth tone of the major scale as its tonic. This changes the semitones (half steps) between the second and third tones and the fifth and sixth tones creating a scale formula of Whole – Half – Whole – Whole – Half – Whole – Whole.

Sixteenth Note: A note having the time duration of one sixteenth of the time duration of a whole note.

Syncopation: Deliberate altering of the meter or pulse of a composition by a temporarily shifting the accent to a weak beat or an off-beat.

Turnaround: A short phrase at the end of a progression that brings the player back to the beginning of the song in a smooth transition.

Arpeggio: The notes of a chord played separately.

Octave: An interval spanning seven diatonic degrees (eleven half-steps). An octave above C would be C.

Root Note: The tonic or fundamental note of a chord. The note which gives a chord or scale its letter name.

Caged System: A "five shape" contiguous sequence that spans the fretboard of a guitar based off of the C, A, G, E and D (major, minor, dominant 7th, etc.) open chord forms.

Bi-Dextral Hammer On: Also known as "tapping." Bi-Dextral Hammer Ons are performed by using the left and right hands to perform wide stretch hammer ons and pull offs.

Blues Tri-Tone: The interval of a sharped fourth (augmented fourth, enharmonically spelled as a diminished fifth). This interval was known as the "devil in music" in the Medieval era because it is the most dissonant sound in the scale. This note is usually added to a minor pentatonic scale to give it a bluesy sound.

Melody: A succession of musical tones. It represents the linear or horizontal aspect of music.

Dominant 7th Chord: A chord constructed with the 1st = 3rd – 5th – and b7 degrees of a major scale. Also known as a 7th chord.

Greensleeves

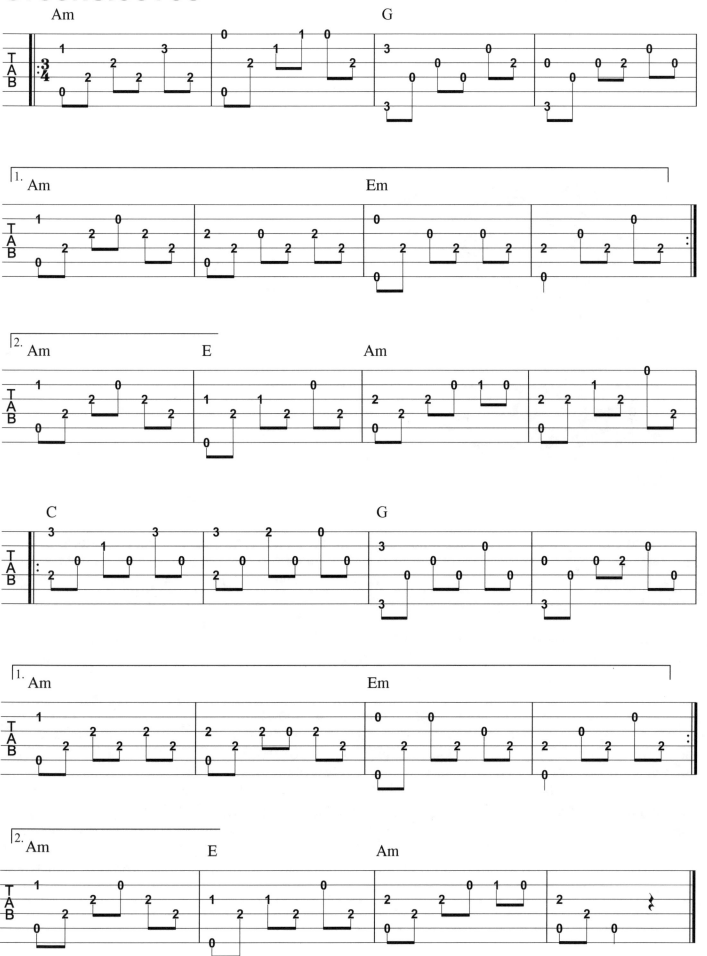

About the Author

John McCarthy
Creator of
The Rock House Method

John is the creator of The Rock House Method®, the world's leading musical instruction system. Over his 25 plus year career, he has written, produced and/or appeared in more than 100 instructional products. Millions of people around the world have learned to play music using John's easy-to-follow, accelerated programs.

John is a virtuoso musician who has worked with some of the industry's most legendary entertainers. He has the ability to break down, teach and communicate music in a manner that motivates and inspires others to achieve their dreams of playing an instrument.

As a musician and songwriter, John blends together a unique style of rock, metal, funk and blues in a collage of melodic compositions. Throughout his career, John has recorded and performed with renowned musicians including Doug Wimbish (Joe Satriani, Living Colour, The Rolling Stones, Madonna, Annie Lennox), Grammy Winner Leo Nocentelli, Rock & Roll Hall of Fame inductees Bernie Worrell and Jerome "Big Foot" Brailey, Freekbass, Gary Hoey, Bobby Kimball, David Ellefson (founding member of seven time Grammy nominee Megadeth), Will Calhoun (B.B. King, Mick Jagger and Paul Simon), Gus G of Ozzy and many more.

To get more information about John McCarthy, his music and instructional products visit Rock-HouseSchool.com.